The Conditioned Origin of Meaning

Takenori Takahashi

Copyright ©2009 Takenori Takahashi
ISBN 978-0-615-26796-8
Library of Congress Control Number: 2008943312

Edited by Michael J. Carr
Design & layout by Val Sherer, Personalized Publishing Services
Cover & index by Paula Hendricks, Cinnabar Bridge
   www. cinnabarbridge.com

Contents

1

Introduction: Linguistically Guilty?

I once analyzed several Japanese *shukanshi* (weekly) magazine headlines that deceived the reader by creating false negative impressions. The usual trick of these headlines is to manipulate the reader's associations. In one case, the magazine waged a malicious campaign to smear a person's reputation by running a long series of articles with highly sensational and misleading headlines. Below is a translation of one of those headlines and a summary of the article. (Although the headline is slightly modified to make it understandable in translation, it is faithful to the original in that it misleads the reader in the same way.)

(1) TWO FEMALE STUDENTS—A HEADACHE FOR PROFESSOR YAMAMOTO (Note: *Yamamoto* is one of the most common family names in Japan.)

(2)   Rumor is that two female students in Professor
      Yamamoto's seminar class are on bad terms. This must
      be causing a headache for him.

My original intent in writing this book was to demonstrate
that the headline's editor is "linguistically guilty" of libel. Why
the editor of this headline in particular? Because the headline is
emblematic of the type of misleading caption frequently used
in certain *shukanshi* magazines. Moreover, while each day millions of people in Japan read *shukanshi* magazines, millions
more come into contact with those magazines' *headlines*, in
newsstands and on posters hanging in the commuter trains. So
the influence of this kind of headline goes far beyond the magazine's actual readership.

I soon realized that linguistically proving the editor's guilt
would be no easy task. First of all, what, exactly, does it mean
to prove something linguistically? Consider the following example:

(3)   John promised to watch the baby for Mary. John
      decided to talk to a friend on the phone. The baby
      crawled outside and fell into the swimming pool and
      nearly drowned. (Dyer, Flowers, and Wang 1992)

Now, suppose that John tries to reject Mary's accusation of
irresponsibility by saying, "I am not irresponsible. I agreed to
watch the baby, and I did. I watched the baby crawl out of the
crib. I watched him crawl to the pool, and I watched him fall
in. You wanted me to watch the baby, and that is exactly what I
did" (Dyer, Flowers, and Wang 1992). Obviously, John is trying
to hide behind sophistry, but ethically he's guilty. Now, suppose
further that the near-drowning incident causes mental impair-

ments to the baby, and this blossoms into a court battle. John will lose the legal battle, of course.

In the eyes of the law, John is certain to be regarded as guilty of gross negligence at the very least. But is he equally guilty from a linguistic point of view? Yes, emphatically. But "linguistically guilty" of *what* exactly? And how can we prove it?

The word "watch" does have the meaning that John contends—his argument suggests that he took the word literally in its primary, most basic sense. But that was not the meaning intended by Mary. If we are willing to take John's argument seriously, the problem lies in the fact that the same word meant one thing to Mary and quite another to John. Does it follow, then, that the root of the problem is the ambiguity of the English language, and that the baby is the unavoidable victim of this "language defect"? The answer is no, because ambiguity is a fundamental and intrinsic feature of all natural languages. In fact, language is *never* free of ambiguity, and we cannot eliminate the ambiguity without eliminating language itself. To communicate using language is to manage ambiguity; thus, John can't pin the blame on the lexical ambiguity of "watch." The issue here is whether each party handled this ambiguity as any reasonable member of their linguistic community would have.

Let's assume that Mary asked John to babysit the child, by telling him, "Watch the baby for me, will you?" We now must ask the following question:

(4)   Did Mary make completely explicit what she wanted to convey?

But this isn't the right question, because…

(5)   Strictly and theoretically speaking, no human
      language, spoken or written, can ever be "completely"
      explicit.

Consider this interaction:

(6)   *Diner:* May I have coffee, please?
      Waiter: Will that be beans, grounds, or liquid? And
      what about the amount? A drop, a cup, a gallon, a
      sack, a barrel, or a shipping container?

Just to illustrate the point, let's suppose (a) that the waiter is not intentionally trying to be difficult and that his questions are genuine and sincere; and (b) that the diner needs to make herself clear to the waiter (without expressing her annoyance). If I were the diner, I might reply, "Give me a cup of *liquid* coffee. Not a spoonful of coffee grounds, a bushel of coffee beans, or an option on coffee futures. Okay?" But what if the waiter returns with a half-filled cup of coffee? I would have to say to him something like, "I want *five-sixths* of a cup of coffee, rather than one-half or two-thirds of a cup." But then again, what if he serves it lukewarm, or boiling hot? This time I would need to say, "I want five-sixths of a cup of liquid coffee with a temperature somewhere between 158 and 162 degrees Fahrenheit." This seems very clear, and no further specification appears to be necessary. But what if he brings me coffee that has been boiling for several hours and has the consistency of mud?

Theoretically, there is no end to this "what if" process. And the same is true for any other linguistic exchange. In other words, it is impossible to articulate in explicit language every conceivable detail and particularity of anything. Therefore, we must ultimately rely on the hearer's ability to *infer*. So what we really need to know is this:

(7)   Was Mary clear enough for John to infer the meaning
      that she wanted to convey?

How does a normal person determine the meaning that
Mary attaches to "watch"? Since the word alone provides no clue
to which of its possible meanings should be selected, a normal
person must figure it out by inference. What, then, is the content
of that inference, how is the inference drawn, and what kind of
knowledge does a normal person use to infer Mary's meaning
of "watch"?

We normally take in the meaning of a group of words as a
coherent whole; that is, we interpret the group together rather
than interpreting its component parts separately. John promised
to "*watch* the baby." He says that he "*watched* the baby crawl to
the pool," as he promised to do. But we don't watch a baby near
the edge of a swimming pool in the same way that we watch, for
example, a diver on a springboard. We know that "watch" has a
different meaning in each group of words (i.e., "watch a baby at
the edge of a swimming pool" and "watch a diver on a springboard").

What, then, do we know about a baby? How do we relate
this knowledge to Mary's request to "watch the baby for me"?
Based on our knowledge of babies, what do we expect from the
situation where the baby is at the edge of the pool, and how
would a responsible person respond to such a situation?

John's argument sounds as if the hearer had the last word in
deciding the meaning of a word. But this is unacceptable. Just
imagine the chaos and confusion in a society where the hearer
has the luxury of interpreting language as he wishes. But then,
if we are to be thus constrained in our interpretations, to whom

does meaning belong? How can we answer these questions linguistically and make John acknowledge his guilt?

As I said, my original intent in writing this book was to prove that the editor of the headline in (1) is linguistically guilty, and that remains the underlying purpose of this work. However, in the process of getting at that editor's linguistic guilt, I had to grapple with some of the most fundamental questions imaginable: What is meaning, and where does it reside? What is language? What is human cognition? What is human nature? And the most fundamental, most crucial of all: What is the right question to ask? This little book is my humble attempt to answer these questions.

Language is a double-edged sword. It can be used either to inform or to mislead, to illuminate the truth or distort it, to unite people or divide them. Never underestimate the power of language.

A famous Buddhist parable describes the Buddha land and hell.

(8)   Someone goes to Hell and finds that everyone there
      is suffering because they cannot eat even though each
      has a sumptuous meal right in front of them. The
      reason they can't eat is that their chopsticks are longer
      than their arms, so they cannot put the food into their
      mouths. The person then goes to the Buddha land.
      There, again, the chopsticks are longer than people's
      arms. But everyone is content. Why? It's because they
      take turns feeding each other. (Ikeda et al. 2002)

The Buddha land and hell are our own creation. "[T]he difference between Hell and Buddhahood is not one of environment. The difference lies solely in the hearts of those dwelling in these realms" (Ikeda et al. 2002).

Language is a powerful tool. As I wrote this book, I continued to ask myself, what is the appropriate attitude for using the power of language? This question reflects the underlying theme, or subtext, that runs through the book.

2

On the Nature of Meaning: The Starting Point

What is the true nature of meaning? Where does meaning exist or reside? In what ways does it exist? How does it arise? Is it constructed, or is it discovered? Is it substantial or insubstantial? The list of questions related to meaning could go on and on, and there are no generally agreed answers. Indeed, the realm of meaning is so full of mysteries, it seems to keep getting further away with every attempt I make to apprehend it. With every answer, a myriad of questions arises, and instead of getting clarity, I find myself steered in the direction of ever greater complexity.

Still, having begun the search, I am determined to see it through to whatever resolution awaits. I will start this journey into the unknown world of meaning, from where I am now, and will keep moving forward, steadily and tenaciously, one step at a time.

The following sections are discussions intended to serve as starting points, or stepping-stones, for exploring the nature of meaning.

Emergence of Word Meaning

How does meaning arise in language? To approach this question, we could start with my introspection on the meaning(s) of a concrete lexical item—namely, the word "kick."

The monosemy position (Ruhl 1989) holds that "kick" has a single, highly abstract meaning, from which multiple concrete meanings can be derived as its contextual variants. In contrast, the polysemy position is skeptical of the existence of such a core, or unified, meaning of "kick" and instead argues that the word carries a set of independent, discrete meanings. Our concern here, however, is not what meaning(s) "kick" has, but this: How does *any* meaning of "kick" emerge?

First, let us assume that "kick" does indeed have a single, monosemous meaning. Such a meaning, however, does not seem to have direct access to my conscious awareness; that is, it fails to project a tangible image of itself onto my mental screen. Therefore, my subjective observation is that although it may exist theoretically, this aspect of the meaning of "kick" is too abstract to emerge on the surface level of consciousness.

Next, suppose that there exists a set of distinct meanings for "kick" and that I am tasked with deciding which meaning comes to my mind at the outset. If I am presented with "kick" in isolation, without any context, the first meaning I think of is

(9)   to hit or strike with the foot.

But after careful thought, (9) proves to be merely a paraphrase of the meaning and tells us nothing of how the meaning arises. Strictly speaking, the meaning in question does not originate in rewording the meaning, nor does it coincide with the act of thinking of paraphrasing words such as "hit" or "foot." In the process of the emergence of the meaning, there is something that precedes the act of rewording or paraphrasing.

When I come into contact with the word "kick," I find myself forming a vague mental image that could be described as

(10) somebody kicks something.

In other words, a very general instantiation involving a kicking action is activated.

Now, while it is true this instantiation is characterized by its high degree of vagueness or abstractness, it nonetheless is not completely empty or void. Indeed, it has more concreteness than first appears. For example, "kick" can function as a noun (e.g., "a powerful *kick*"). Example (10) shows that my instantiation has occurred in the context of "kick" being assumed to be a verb. Let me further point out that although "kick" can be an intransitive verb (e.g., "The toddler *kicked* angrily while being bathed."), (10) does not illustrate the intransitive, or objectless, sense of the verb. To put it another way, my instantiation of "kick" has occurred in connection not only with its agent (kicker) but also with its theme (kickee). Also, note that my instantiation is more specific than, say,

(11) X kicks Y.

In (11), both arguments of "kick" are left undefined in terms of their semantic features, whereas in (10), the agent argument is associated with the [human] feature (somebody), and the theme argument with the [inanimate] feature (something).

From the above observation, we can propose the following tentative conclusions: (a) When "kick" is presented to me as a stimulus, what seems to me to be a "typical" meaning of the word emerges; and (b) the emergence of this meaning is coupled with the activation of what, again, seems to be a "typical" kicking scenario, namely, "human kicks inanimate."

I must add, however, that the mental image of a "typical" kicking scenario can vary from person to person, and it can also fluctuate individually over time. For example, if I were a professional kickboxer, the "human kicks human" scenario would probably emerge as the most typical one. Similarly, if I had watched a kickboxing match on TV just before writing this section, the "human kicks human" scenario would be more readily activated and, as a result, might be felt as more typical than other scenarios.

Be that as it may, the typical kicking scenario for me at the moment of this writing is "human kicks inanimate," and with the activation of this scenario comes the sense that the meaning of "kick" has emerged in me.

So far, we have discussed the emergence of the meaning of "kick" in a situation where the word occurs in isolation. Now let us deal with instances where "kick" occurs in a sentence. Look at the following examples from Anderson and Shifrin (1980):

(12) a. The punter kicked the ball.

    b. The baby kicked the ball.

    c. The golfer kicked the ball.

The sentences in (12) share the same verb ("kicked") with the same object noun phrase ("the ball"). And yet, the meaning of "kicked" cannot be said to be identical in the three examples, because in each case the verb provokes a different instantiation in terms of the speed and strength and intent of the kicking motion or the overall manner of the kicking action.

To what, then, do we attribute the difference in instantiation? Since the sentences in (12) share the same verb phrase ("kicked the ball"), we could begin by saying that the difference is due to the different subject noun phrases supplied along with the verb phrase. For example, the punter and the baby are naturally expected to have quite different physical and motor capacities, and consequently, the mental visualizations of the kicking actions performed by them are quite different.

But note that the different subject noun phrases also have an effect on the instantiation of the postverbal object noun phrase ("the ball"). For example, when reading (12a), most people would assume the ball to be a football, whereas in (12b), the ball implied seems to be a brightly colored, inflated plastic ball (Anderson and Shifrin 1980) or a light, soft, squishy rubber ball.

Now, note that how "the ball" is instantiated influences in turn our perception of the entire event described in the sentence as a whole. And this, in turn, has an effect on the instantiation of the verb "kick." Usually, a "kicking" scenario involves not only a kicker, a kickee, and some degree of motor exertion, but also a location or situation where the kicking takes place. In (12a), for example, the instantiation of the "ball" as a "football" is likely to elicit a mental scenario of the punter kicking the ball in a football game. By the same token, in (12c), the subject noun phrase ("the golfer") invites an assumption that the ball the golfer kicked is a golf ball and that the kicking happened during a game of golf. This assumption eventually influences the formation of the mental image—or the instantiation—of how the golfer kicked the ball. It is a breach of rules or etiquette for a golfer to kick the ball, and therefore, (12c) evokes an image of the golfer kicking a golf ball in a "cheating" or "angry" way.

Let's look at our example again:

(12) a. The punter kicked the ball.

When I first encountered this sentence over twenty years ago, I had no knowledge of what a "punter" was and, therefore, had no clear idea of the likely speed and strength of the kicking motion, or the manner of the kicking action performed by the punter, nor could I get a clear mental image of the size, weight, or shape of the ball. Then I looked up the word "punter" in the dictionary and found it to mean "(football) a person who kicks the football by dropping it from the hands and contacting it with the foot before it hits the ground." And it was with this "knowledge" from the dictionary that the meaning of "kicked" in (12a) emerged before me. This phenomenon makes me aware that the meaning of "kicked" in "X kicked the ball" emerges depending not only on what X is but also on the *reader's knowledge* of X. One could argue that the meaning of "kicked" was out there in sentence (12a) regardless of my knowledge of "punter" two decades ago. But note once again that our concern here is in *how meaning emerges*. Before I gained the knowledge of what a "punter" is, the meaning of "kicked" in (12a) existed, but in a latent or dormant state that was not actualized in me.

So far, so good. But what do I mean when I say "the *reader's knowledge*"? For this, we turn to Kitchell (2000).

(13) a. The baby kicked the ball and laughed.
　　　 The golfer kicked the ball and laughed.
　　　 The punter kicked the ball and laughed.

　　b. Yet think what the sentence would mean to a native of New Zealand who was trained in British English in a small school somewhere away from American television. He or she would have a sense of "ball" of course, but not of "punter" unless as a slightly derogatory word or as referring to someone who propels a boat with a pole. Even if he were told that one of the games was "football," he would have entirely different culturally determined views (schemata) of what was going on, since "football" to such a person is our "soccer." (Kitchell 2000)

As Kitchell shows, "knowledge" of the meaning of language fluctuates among different people. With this in mind, let us return to the earlier example:

(12) b. The baby kicked the ball.

I showed this sentence to my wife, who had read and spoken little English during the twenty-five years since she graduated from university. Her first reaction on reading it was,

(14) "Well, the sentence doesn't make sense to me. Babies can't even walk—how can they kick a ball?"

This comment prompted me to do some Internet research on what "baby" really means. Below are some of the relevant results from a 2006 search using such keywords as "define: baby," "baby is defined as," "baby means," and so on:

(15) a. A very young child (birth to one year) who has not yet begun to walk or talk

b. A child under one year who is too young to be able to sit on a seat or walk

c. A very young child, especially one who has not yet begun to walk or talk

d. A broad term that can mean anything from newborn to toddler age

e. On this site, the word "baby" means any child from birth to age four. "Newborn" refers to babies under three months of age. Infants are babies from three months to one year. Toddlers are babies from one year to four years of age.

Based on (15), I would say my wife knew the word "baby" in its narrow sense, and with this in mind, here is the conversation between us that followed:

(16) a. *Me:* But this sentence is from an academic paper published in America.

b. *My wife:* Well, then, maybe the baby was very happy and was kicking his arms and legs cheerfully on the blanket on the floor when his foot hit against the ball, which happened to be close by.

It is interesting to notice that in my wife's construal, the baby in (12b) kicked the ball *unintentionally.* But what is more interesting is to analyze the process of how the nonvolitional meaning of "kicked" in "kicked the ball" emerged. In my analysis, it emerged as the result of the following chain of conditions:

(17) a. I *informed* my wife that (12a) is from an academic paper published in America.

b. This "information" led her to *believe* that (12a) must make sense semantically.

c. This belief led her to *want* to make meaning out of (12a)

d. This desire to make meaning led her to create the scenario that she provided in (16).

e. This "scenario creation" occurred in a way that agreed with her "knowledge," or definition, of the word "baby" without her ever questioning its validity.

Hence the emergence of the nonvolitional meaning of "kicked" in "kicked the ball."

So how does meaning arise? The more I seek the answer to this question, the more I feel invited to pay attention to the "conditions" that help or influence the emergence of meaning.

Emergence of "Word" as Word

The phrase "the meaning of language" presupposes that language *has* meaning and, therefore, that meaning resides in language. What, then, we might ask, is "language" in the first place? Language is a system of arbitrary "signs" created and learned by humans and used for human communication. These signs are considered to have "forms" (and meanings).

(18) Linguistic **form** concerns the way a linguistic expression sounds (for spoken language) or looks (for written or signed language) or how a linguistic expression is produced. Form includes not only the basic units of sound (for spoken language), characters (for written language), and gestural units (for signed

language), but also larger patterns consisting of these units (words, phrases, sentences, etc.) as well as the way these patterns are arranged. It also includes pitch and loudness (for spoken language), punctuation (for written language), and facial expressions (for signed language). (Gasser 2003)

According to Gasser, in written language, linguistic form concerns the way a linguistic expression *looks*. Let's consider the word "bark," for example. We consider it a linguistic sign, that is, a "word," because we perceive it as a *linguistic* form.

Now, for the sake of simplifying the discussion, let's suppose that the earth suddenly became empty of all humans—what would happen to the *linguistic* form "bark"? It would cease to exist, because there would be no creatures left on the earth that could perceive it as a linguistic form. The surviving animals might see it as a form, or shape, or marks (made with ink, pencil, or other means), but they would not see it as a *linguistic* form.

Reid uses the Venus de Milo as an example:

(19) If an extra-terrestrial traveller, which had never encountered humans, were to arrive inside the Louvre Museum one night while it was empty of humans and were to approach the statue, that traveller would not see it as a work of art. It would not even see it as human. The statue would be simply an unusually shaped stone. (Reid 2001)

So, returning to the example of "bark," it would not be far-fetched to conclude that "bark" as a *linguistic form* exists with humans as a condition. In other words, "bark" as a linguistic form requires for its existence the existence of humans as its

17

"perceivers." It is not an objective entity that resides, or can be located, inside "bark" itself. It is a construct that depends on humans as a condition and that manifests itself *in response* to that condition.

Now suppose that fifty years after the extinction of the human race, an extraterrestrial intelligence that could read and understand English came to the earth and encountered "bark." In that case, it would follow that "bark's" *linguistic* form would reemerge.

At this point, a new question arises. Where was "'bark' as a linguistic form" during those fifty years? Or, to put it another way, where was it during the time when the condition supporting its existence was absent? Was it *absolutely* nonexistent? Did it become extinct concomitantly with the extinction of humans, or did it continue to exist in some way, in some different plane or dimension? The fifty years, in a sense, is a "black box."

Again, was "'bark' as a linguistic form" absolutely nonexistent? That does not seem to be the case, because, with the appearance of the extraterrestrial intelligence, it reemerged. If it had not continued to exist in some way, it could not have emerged. But then, in what way *did* it exist?

What is certain is that "bark" itself was there before, during, and after the "black box" period of time, and that "'bark' *as a linguistic form*" is one of the different *aspects* of "bark"; thus, these two are inseparable. Based on this fact, we can conclude that they both existed throughout all three periods of time. And then, based on this conclusion, we should assume that during the black-box period of time, the latter ("'bark' *as a linguistic form*") existed with the former ("bark" itself) as a "potential" that could reemerge into a manifest state if the former ("bark" itself) should encounter the right condition(s). Thus, "bark," "'bark' as a linguistic form," and their "perceivers" are all three inextricably related.

Before closing this section, note that the progression of thought traced above would be equally valid when we deal with the question of the "meaning" of language. We will explore this in some detail later. For now, we need only acknowledge the following points:

(20) a. The meaning of language exists with its "perceiver" as condition. For example, when in contact with the right perceiver, the form (or shape, or mark) "bark" manifests itself as a *linguistic form* and, thus, as a *linguistic sign* or *linguistic unit* called a "word": hence the existence of the *meaning* of "bark" (whatever it is).

b. In the absence of the right perceiver, however, the "meaning" of language exists *with* "language" in the state of potentiality.

Two Types of Environment

Suppose a dog bangs on a computer keyboard, and the string of letters appearing on the screen happens to read "bark." What observations can we make about this situation? First, we can say,

(21) The dog does not mean anything by the word "bark." (It is not even aware that "bark" is a linguistic sign with meaning.)

Looking at it from the other side (that is, from the stand-point of "bark"), we can also safely say,

(22) The word "bark," for its part, doesn't mean anything to the dog, either.

The word exists there on the screen (by accident), but to the dog, it cannot reveal its aspect as a linguistic sign, and so it fails to function as a word. A generalization of this is that a word may have meaning but cannot *express* that meaning on its own or by itself.

Now, if an English-speaker sees the same string of letters, "bark's" linguistic meaning arises. So far, so good. But why is that so, and what is the mechanism behind it? "Bark" invokes its meaning as a linguistic sign when it comes into contact with an English-speaker—not because it can express its meaning on its own or by itself, but because it can *stimulate* the English-speaker. From this, we can generalize the following:

(23) a. The meaning of a word emerges out of the word as a result of the word's functioning and serving as a stimulus for the activation of its own (dormant) meaning.

b. The meaning of a word emerges and becomes active in a person as a result of that person's response to the stimulus of the word.

Thus, it follows that...

(24) a. Both a word and a person constitute conditions for the meaning of the word to arise.

    b. The meaning of a word arises as a result of the interplay of these conditions (that is, the word itself and a person).

With this in mind, let's explore another possibility:

(25) He *barked* his shin.

Very often a word has more than one meaning, and the verb "bark" (the stem of "barked") in (25) is no exception. For example, in isolation, it has two meanings that spring readily to mind: (intransitive) make the short, loud cry of a dog; and (transitive) rub off the skin of. In other words, for me, at the time of this writing, the verb "bark" has two salient *possible* meanings and therefore has the *potential* to give rise to either of them. But "bark" in (25) seems quite unambiguous; almost automatically I take it to mean "rub off the skin of." How, then, does this meaning instead of the other emerge?

(26) a. The pronoun "he" (along with its variant "his") refers to a person. It can also refer to an animal, including a dog (e.g., "Your *dog* is well trained; he is a good guard dog.").

    b. In the absence of clear evidence to the contrary, it is reasonable to presume, in (25), that "he" and "his" are *coreferential* (i.e., he$_i$ barked his$_i$ shin.)

    c. "Shin" means the front part of the human leg, between the knee and the ankle.

    d. "Bark" is used as an *intransitive* verb when it means "make the short, loud cry of a dog."

    e. The above (a–d) are my mind's response to the stimulus of the sentence "He barked his shin."

These conditions together support and contribute to the natural and rational emergence of the meaning of "bark" in (25): "rub off the skin of." Although the conditions stated in (26) function as a unified whole, for analytical purposes they can be viewed as a combination of two types of environments: linguistic and extralinguistic. From this standpoint, we can interpret (26) in the following general terms:

(27) Environments that surround a word and support or influence the emergence of the meaning of the word:

a. Linguistic environment in which the word in question occurs—the meaning of the word emerges dependent on the other words around it. In other words, co-occurring words serve as condition factors for the emergence of the meaning of the word. The meaning of the word is determined by its semantic relationships with the other words, as well as the syntactic structure in which the word occurs.

b. Extralinguistic environment:

The meaning of the word emerges dependent on how a person responds to the word and its linguistic environment. Again, the word and its linguistic environment cannot express the meaning of the word on their own or by themselves; they function simply as linguistic stimuli.

The Arising and Cessation of Meaning in the Realm of Linguistic Environment

In (25), "he," "barked," "his," and "shin" all share the same linguistic environment, and the environment in this case is a linguistic unit called a *sentence* ("He barked his shin."). Of course, there are other units of language, which can be smaller or larger than a sentence. For example, "his shin" is a unit called a *phrase*.

(28) his shin

In (28), the referential meaning of "his" is dependent on "shin" because the meaning of "shin" narrowly constrains the domain of possible referents of "his" to humans. And when (28) is embedded in the sentence (25), this referential meaning of "his" remains unchanged.

But there are also cases where a constituent of a unit changes its meaning when the unit is embedded in a larger unit or environment:

(29) a. He barked his shin.

    b. He was a remarkable ventriloquist. First, he made it seem that the cat was barking. Then he made the parrot bark. Then he barked a monkey, and then a shoe, then his hand, and then he barked his shin. (Ziff 1972)

A word has more than one meaning as potentials. In the case of "bark," "make the short, loud cry of a dog" and "rub off the skin of" are two of several possible meanings of the word. In (29a), the latter meaning instead of the former is activated. No matter how closely we look at the sentence, or how many minute pieces we cut it into, nowhere within it can we find the former meaning. This is because (29a) as a whole forms a linguistic environment that *constrains* the activation or actualization of the former meaning potential of "bark." And note that this environment merely constrains but does not really eradicate or kill the potential itself.

With a slight modification of viewpoint, the above discussion of "meaning potential" can be applied to sentence (29a) as a unified whole. The meaning of (29a) is that

(30) some person rubbed off the skin of the lower front part of his leg.

But we cannot decide that this is the *only* meaning that (29a) can ever take on. There simply is no proof for such a claim; therefore, we may conclude,

(31) Although (30) is the most likely and probable meaning of (29a), it is still only one of the possible meanings of (29a).

And we can use (29b) as proof. If (29a) has one and only one meaning and that meaning is (30), then (30) should always emerge as the meaning of (29a), regardless of the linguistic environment that (29a) is in. But in (29b), in which (29a) is embedded in the form of a clause, "he barked his shin" takes on a meaning very different from that of (30). In other words, the identical set of words, arranged in exactly the same order, can have two entirely different meanings.

As far as the *linguistic* environment is concerned, in (29a) the set of words "he barked his shin" makes up the largest environment for itself and its constituents. By contrast, in (29b) the same set of words occurs as a constituent of a larger environment and receives influence from that environment, and the influence eventually reaches "bark."

What is important here is that our observation about (29a) can—and should—be applied equally to (29b). Under different environments or conditions, it, too, can take on a different meaning, and, in response to the emergence of that meaning, "he barked his shin" can regain (30) as its meaning—or yet another potential meaning can unfold.

In this way, even in the realm of linguistic environment alone, the arising of meaning is an interactive, not an isolated, process. Meaning arises from various "conditions" and most often is a result of the interplay of those conditions. In other words,

(32) Meaning m emerges because of a combination of conditions that are present to support its emergence.

On the other side of the coin,

(33) Meaning m disappears with the cessation of the combination of conditions that supported its emergence.

Therefore,

(34) The arising of meaning m is a phenomenon that occurs with, and out of, the temporary union or integration of the conditions that support its arising.

Consider again the examples in (29), repeated here:

(35) a. He barked his shin.

b. He was a remarkable ventriloquist. First, he made it seem that the cat was barking. Then he made the parrot bark. Then he barked a monkey, and then a shoe, then his hand, and then he barked his shin.

"Barked" in (35a) means "rubbed off the skin of," and this meaning arises dependent on the environment in which "barked" occurs. This environment, which is "he barked his shin," forms a united whole or is formed by an organic union or integration of four words. This union is temporary, not something fixed and absolute, because it can become loose or disintegrate when the environment is embedded and merged into a larger environment. One such case is (35b). Here we lose the integrative power that used to hold the four words in (35a) in such a state of union as to support the emergence of "rubbed off the skin of" as the meaning of "barked." In (35b), "he barked his shin" means "he made it seem that his shin was barking," and therefore, "barked" means "was making *woof, woof* sounds." These meanings of "he barked his shin" and "barked" arise out of the temporary union of the environment in which the clause and the word occur. If all words in (35b) that precede "he barked his shin" are removed, those four words regain the integrative power they held before the other words were added. In this way, the meaning of language dynamically appears and disappears in response to the integration and disintegration of the conditions that support its emergence.

Convergence of the Two Environments

A linguistic unit such as a word, phrase, clause, sentence, or text—in short, language—has meaning potentials. However, language cannot actualize its meaning potentials on its own or by itself; rather, it functions as a stimulus for its meaning to transform from potential to actual. That is, language serves as a condition for its own meaning potentials to emerge into a manifest state. Another important condition for the actualization of meaning potentials is the "recipient" of the linguistic stimuli. As we know, animals cannot perceive human language as we do. And so, for them, its meaning potentials just lie there in a state of dormancy. But how about humans—can we actualize those meaning potentials? Well…yes and no. Look at (36) below. I remember my reaction when I read one of the three vignettes in (36) on the

Internet for the first time. (I cannot remember exactly which one it was; indeed, it may have been some other version of the story, which had the same effect. For our purposes here, we can continue the discussion on the assumption that it was [36a].)

(36) a. One day, a father and his son went for a drive. Unfortunately, they had a traffic accident. The father died, and the son was carried into a hospital. On seeing the boy, the surgeon said, "I can't operate, because he is my own son!"

   b. This morning, a father and his son were driving along the highway to work, when they were involved in a horrible accident. The father was killed, and the son was quickly driven to the hospital, severely injured. When the boy was taken into the operating room, the surgeon exclaimed, "Oh, my God, this is my son!"

   c. A father and his son are in an automobile. They have an accident. The father is killed, and the son is rushed to the hospital. A surgeon is called in to perform an intricate operation. When the operation is successfully completed, the surgeon looks at the boy's face for the first time and says, "Why, that's my son!"

When I first read (36a), my reaction was that something was missing between the story and me. I was able to translate it correctly into my first language (Japanese), and that meant, as far as linguistic (lexical, syntactic, and semantic) knowledge was concerned, that I had no problem interpreting it. Also, (36a) seemed to me to be an example of what we linguists call a "text"; that is, it did not seem to lack integrative power that binds its constituents together as a unified whole. And yet, the unified meaning of the text did not reach me, due to some kind of barrier between myself and the text. Then, after struggling with (36a) for a while, I realized that the barrier was my strong assumption about the sex of the "surgeon" in the story. I had taken it for granted that the surgeon was male. When I realized that the surgeon was the boy's mother, the story made sense to me—that is, its integrated meaning emerged in me.

This reading experience of mine implies,

(37) A human being serves as a condition for actualizing the meaning potentials of language, by receiving and responding to linguistic stimuli. But at the actual scene of the emergence of meaning, a variety of other conditions are found to be at work and to affect the way language is processed. These conditions are the conditions that coexist with human beings or pertain to human nature, and they may support or hinder the emergence of meaning.

With this in mind, let us consider (36a) again. I was eventually able to make sense of the story, but it was as a result of certain conditions being met. My failure at the outset was due to my false assumption that the surgeon was male. If I had not become aware of my preconceived assumption, I might simply have dismissed (36a) as nonsense. If this had been the case, the meaning potential of (36a) would not have been actualized (or rather, it would not even have been recognized). The fact was, I thought it must make sense in some way. This thought prompted me to strive to make it meaningful, and as a result of this effort, I realized my preconceived assumption about the surgeon's gender and understood that the surgeon was female.

Since my realizing that the surgeon was female seems to have led directly to the emergence of the unified meaning of (36a), we could say that this was the "deciding" condition for (36a) to actualize its meaning potential. But the satisfaction or realization of this condition is supported by that of the antecedent (or attendant, or supportive) conditions. For example, my desire and effort to make sense of (36a) was motivated, and therefore supported, by my assumption that (36a) must somehow make sense. Also, there was no guarantee that my effort would bear fruit. I might have ended up abandoning my effort, deciding that (36a) was too difficult for me to make sense of. But in fact, I did not give up and was lucky enough to get the meaning. All these conditions are connected in a seamless way. Therefore, it is probably more accurate to say that the deciding condition was the integrated functioning of these conditions.

Now let's look a little more closely at my initial assumption about the gender of the surgeon. This assumption is not something that resides in the word itself; it is what I had brought to it. We could say that at the start of my reading of (36a), I approached the word "surgeon" with a gender bias toward males. Here I would like to discuss some of the characteristics of this bias as they pertain to the emergence of the meaning of (36a).

First, when I was caught up in this bias, the meaning of (36a) was submerged behind the text; and sometime later, with my realization of the bias, the meaning emerged out of the text. Here is the generalization of this phenomenon: A bias existing in a person can block the actualization of the meaning potential of a text. However, the influence of that bias is not something fixed and absolute; if we become aware of the bias, we "get out of" its influence, and the meaning emerges. Moreover, the "getting out" process can be relatively short.

Next, where did my bias come from? Of course, we could say that I myself am the source of the bias. But then, what am I, and what makes me up? I am what I was *born as*—a human, male, Asian, Japanese, and so on—and so I cannot sever myself from these conditions. Also, I am what I have *become*, and so I cannot dissociate myself from my past, from my history. Further, I am part of my *environment* (my family, workplace, community, society, culture, generation, and so on), and so I cannot separate myself from that, either. Therefore, these elements naturally play a role as conditional factors for the formation of my bias. My bias can be rooted in my gender, past experiences, age, occupation, and so on. As an example, let's consider an environmental factor. The following is from the *Tribune* online edition of July 27, 2003:

> (38) Once, a father and his son met with an accident. They were brought to hospital where it was discovered that the son would have to be operated upon. On seeing the boy on the operation table, the surgeon exclaimed, "I can't do this operation. The boy is my son." What could be the relation of the surgeon to the family? When this quiz was placed before a group of men and women, it took them some time to decode the answer. On further investigation it was found that most of them could not guess instantly that the "surgeon" could be a female and the boy's mother. (Bande 2003)

If I belong to the same community as the men and women mentioned in (38), it follows that my bias is shared, at least to some degree, by the people in the community. It is not particular to me, nor is it particular to the male members of the community. Thus, it is also possible to say that my environment is the source of the bias. Actually, *every* environment has a tendency to breed some kinds and degrees of bias.

What is important, however, is that environment is not something fixed and frozen. It can vary over time, among regions, or between individuals (or small groups in a community). For example, suppose I am a female surgeon at one of the many hospitals in the above community, where all the other surgeons happen to be female, too. Chances are fairly good that on reading the same story in (38), I instantly think of a female surgeon.

Next, suppose that I failed to get out of the influence of my bias yet kept on striving to make (36a) meaningful, and that my effort yielded an interpretation that fit into my preconceived assumption. For example, something like this: *Just before her marriage (or even after she married), the boy's mother slept with her boyfriend, and the boy was the result. The surgeon was the boyfriend. After she gave birth to the boy, she told the surgeon about the paternity, but she kept it secret from her husband. The surgeon had watched from a distance as the boy grew up.* Certainly, this is an interpretation based on an unlikely scenario, but the important point is that such a meaning actually can emerge and make sense.

Thus, we see that (36a) is there as a condition and a stimulus waiting for its meaning potentials to be actualized. It awaits an encounter with a condition from the extralinguistic environment—a person—who can respond to the stimulus it provides. However, when the encounter actually takes place, it takes place not in a vacuum but in a concrete situation that is in a state of uncertainty and flux. This is because a person is not a static being but an ever-moving and -evolving process, or an unfolding movement. Also, a human is an entity living and developing in a complex web of biological, physical, psychological, social, cultural, and other kinds of influences, and brings those influences to (36a). In other words, those influences constitute conditions affecting whether, and how, meaning potentials of (36a) are actualized. Here is a simple example: Suppose I am physically fatigued and in no mood to figure out what (36a) means. I take a rest break and then read it again—and successfully figure it out. In this case, we could say that my relative physical and mental fatigue is one of the various conditions affecting actualization of the meaning potentials of (36a). On another front, a slight variation in the wording of (36a) can influence how I respond to the story. The following is one of the story's many variants that one can easily find on the Internet:

(39) A father and his son get in a car accident. The father dies, and the son, in a coma, is rushed off to the hospital for an operation. When he gets there, the *old* surgeon looks at him and says, "I can't operate on this boy; he's my son!" [Emphasis added.]

My assumption about the surgeon's gender may be enhanced by the added adjective "old," and as a result, I may think of a rather unusual scenario that fits my assumption. In this case, my gender bias has resonated with the expression "old surgeon," and my bias, the stimuli from the text (including "old surgeon"), and other conditions are united to actualize one of the meaning potentials of the text. Again, this is a temporal union, because, if "old" is removed, the union can become loose or disintegrate altogether, and a different union of conditions can occur, giving rise to the actualization of another meaning potential.

To conclude this section,

(40) a. Meaning arises through the interaction of the conditions in both realms, that is, conditions in linguistic and extralinguistic environments.

   b. The conditions involved, while distinct, work together as one.

   c. The emergence of meaning is a phenomenon that occurs with, and out of, the temporary union of the conditions involved.

Origin of Meaning

As a student of linguistics rather than philosophy, my main concern in this work is with the meaning of language (more specifically, of *natural* language). Before delving into this particular issue, we need to deal with a fundamental question: Where does meaning originate?

Two Ideas

"Meaning" is a problematic notion with multiple—and often competing—interpretations and explanations. The question of where meaning originates is no exception. We can begin the exploration of this subject by introducing the following descriptions of two relevant but competing ideas, from Stephen Law (2003):

(41) Where Does Meaning Originate?
   Take a look at the following sequence of straight and curved lines.

   I AM HAPPY.

In English these lines mean *I am happy*. But there could be other languages in which this same combination of lines conveys quite a different thought. There might be an alien civilisation for which they mean *my trousers are in tatters* (I don't say this is likely, of course, but it's possible). The lines are in themselves devoid of any particular meaning.

The same is true of other forms of representation, including diagrams, illustrations and samples. They don't have any *intrinsic* representational power or meaning....

What of a simple patch of red? Surely that can mean only one thing: red.

Not so. A red patch might have all sorts of meanings. If the patch is square, for example, then it might mean *red square*. Or it might simply mean *square* (the sample just happens to be red). If the patch is scarlet, then it might be used to represent just that shade of red. Or it could also be used to represent a much wider section of the colour spectrum, such as red, purple, and blue. A red patch might be used to symbolise blood or to warn of danger. I could use a red blob to record in my diary those days on which I ate a chocolate biscuit. In fact, a red match might be used to mean pretty much anything.

The moral is that nothing is intrinsically meaningful. Anything can be used to represent or mean more or less anything under the right conditions.

Meaning as an "Inner" Process

But if nothing *intrinsically* means or represents any-thing, then how do our words and other symbols come by their representational powers? What gives them meaning? The answer, of course, is that we do. But how?

Here's one traditionally popular suggestion.

Suppose that a parrot starts to mimic the expression "I am happy." Of course, the parrot doesn't mean anything by these words. It's probably unaware even that the words have a meaning. On the other hand, when I say "I am happy," I don't just say something: I mean something.

So, although we say the same words, only one of us means something by them. Why is this? Why do I mean something but the parrot doesn't? After all, both the parrot and I engage in *the same outward, observable process.* We both say, "I am happy."

It seems, then, that the essential difference between us must be *hidden.* In meaning something, I must be engaged in an additional process, a process that accompanies the outward process of saying the words, a process that the parrot doesn't engage in. When I say "I am happy," the outward physical process of saying is accompanied by *an inner mental process of meaning.* It is the inner mental process that breathes life into our words and transforms them from mere sounds into significant utterances.

Locke's Theory of Meaning

An example of the view that meaning is essentially "inner" is provided by the seventeenth-century philosopher John Locke.

In Locke's view, the mind is like a container. At birth, the container is empty. Gradually, our senses begin to furnish this inner space with objects. Locke calls these mental objects "Ideas." We have simple Ideas, such as the Idea of the colour red. Locke seems to think of the Idea of red as being a mental image of some sort. We also have complex Ideas that are built out of simple Ideas. For example, my Idea of a snowball fight is made up of simpler Ideas, including those of white, cold, hard and round.

In Locke's view, Ideas form the building blocks of thought. Our thoughts are made up of sequences of Ideas. And words obtain their meaning by standing for these Ideas: "Words in their primary or immediate Signification, stand for nothing, but the Idea in the Mind of him that uses them..." – John Locke, *An Essay Concerning Human Understanding*

The difference between me and the parrot, in Locke's view—the difference that explains why I mean something by and understand what I say and the parrot doesn't—is that, unlike the parrot, I have correlated the outward string of words "I am happy" with the sequence of mental objects. The outward process of saying the words is accompanied by an inner parade of Ideas. No such mental parade takes place inside the mind of the parrot.

This is called the *Ideational theory of meaning*.

How to Pick Out a "Red" Object

The Ideational theory provides an explanation of how we are able to understand and apply a word correctly. For example, suppose I ask you to pick out something red from your environment. No doubt you did so effortlessly. Yet all I gave you were some squiggly lines: "red." How did you know what to do with them?

It seems that in the Ideational theory, something like the following must have happened. You engaged in a sort of internal "looking-up" process. On receiving the word "red," you looked up in your memory—which functions, in effect, as a storehouse of Ideas—the Idea with which you have previously learned to correlate that word. This Idea, a sort of memory image of the colour red, provides you with a template or sample with which other things can be compared. You then compared this Idea with the objects around you until you got a match. You then picked the object.

You may not be conscious of having engaged in such an inner "looking-up" process. But perhaps that is because, for a mature language user like yourself, the process is so quick and habitual that you no longer need to pay it any attention.

A Popular Picture

Down through the centuries, many thinkers have been drawn to the "inner process" model of meaning and understanding sketched out above. Indeed, the inner process model might well strike you as being "just obviously" true. How else, you might wonder, are we to think of meaning and understanding, if not in terms of such processes taking place in the mind? Almost everyone finds themselves drawn to the inner process model when first they start to think about meaning and understanding.

It may surprise you then, to discover that the inner process model is now rejected by the vast majority of philosophers. One of the main reasons for this is the influence of the later work of Wittgenstein. Wittgenstein constructed powerful arguments that show that the inner process model doesn't explain what it's supposed to. Here are two of Wittgenstein's best-known criticisms of the inner process model.

Argument 1: How to Pick the Right Inner Object?

Let's return to the suggestion that to understand a word is to engage in an inner looking-up process. Think about the following scenario:

Pedro runs a paint shop. Pedro receives lots of orders for paint written in English. Unfortunately, Pedro cannot read English. So John, who can, set up a little filing cabinet in Pedro's office. In the cabinet are cards. On each card is a blob of paint. The cards also have labels taped to them. On each label is printed the English word for the colour that appears on the cards. When Pedro gets an order, he simply checks the English colour on the order form against the labels in his file. When he finds the right card, he pulls it out and compares the colour on the card with the tins of paint in his shop. Pedro then dispatches a tin of that colour.

It was suggested a moment ago that a similar looking-up process must explain your ability to apply the term "red" correctly. Only we supposed that the looking-up process must take place *in your mind*. You have a *mental* filing cabinet, if you like—a storehouse of Ideas—in which you have previously filed memory images of colours correlated with their English names. When you received the word "red," you went to your mental filing cabinet and pulled out the right sample. You then compared the objects around you with the memory image until you found the match.

But does this inner looking-up process really explain your ability to pick out those things to which the word "red" applies? Not according to Wittgenstein, who points out that the process actually presupposes what it's supposed to explain. To see why, ask yourself the following question: how did you pick out the right memory image?

"I don't see the problem," you might say. "Why can't I just go to my mental filing cabinet and look up the right mental image, the one I previously correlated with the word 'red'?"

The difficulty is that a mental image is not objective. It's not the sort of thing you might attach a label to and put in a drawer for future reference. Once you're no longer aware of a mental image, it's gone. So when next you want to conjure up a mental image of "red," how do you know what sort of image you are supposed to be imagining? You need already to know what "red" means in order to know that. Yet it was your knowledge of what "red" means that the mental image was supposed to explain.

So the "inner process" explanation of how you are able to apply "red" correctly is circular. It's suggested that you are able to pick out the right external object by comparing it with an inner object. But this takes for granted your ability to pick out the right *inner* object. We've taken for granted precisely the ability we're supposed to be explaining. The situation is quite different when it comes to an *objective* sample, like a piece of coloured card. Pedro doesn't need to know what "red" means in order to find the right coloured sample in his filing cabinet. This is because the word "red" is physically, objectively taped to the right piece of card.

Argument 2: How Does the Inner Object Come by Its Meaning?

Even if you can somehow manage to call up the right memory image without already knowing what "red" means, there remains a problem. The suggestion that words and other signs ultimately come by their meaning by being correlated with inner objects—Ideas—seems satisfactory only while one forgets to ask: and how in turn do these *inner* objects come by *their* meaning?

Suppose that you correlate the word "red" with a mental image of a red square. Do you thereby give "red" a meaning?

No. We have already seen the public samples—a red square painted on a piece of card, for example—can be interpreted in innumerable ways. But exactly the same difficulty arises with respect to mental samples. They are no more *intrinsically* meaningful than are public samples.

Let's suppose, for example, that your mental image is of a scarlet square. Should you then apply "red" only to scarlet objects? Or would an orange object do? Or perhaps your sample just happens to be red, and it really represents squareness. So should you pick out only square objects? And so on. Your mental image fails to provide the answers to any of these questions.

It's clear that we have again gone round in a circle. This time, we have explained how words and other signs come by their meaning only by presupposing that certain signs—the mental ones—*already* have a meaning. So the mystery of how meaning ultimately originates remains.

Round and Round in Circles...

Wittgenstein points out that the explanations provided by the inner process model are circular. The model tries to explain how public words and signs have meaning by appealing to private, inner objects, but then takes the meaning of these inner objects for granted. It also tries to explain how you are able to identify which external objects are "red," but only by presupposing that you already possess the ability to identify which internal objects are "red". Here are two more examples of circular explanations. We once tried to explain how the earth is held up by supposing that it sits on the back of a great animal: an elephant. Of course, this explanation didn't really remove the mystery with which we were grappling, for we then needed to explain what held the elephant up. So we introduced another animal—a turtle—for the elephant to sit on.

But then what did the turtle sit on? Should we have introduced yet another animal to support the turtle, and another animal to support that animal, and so on without end?

The problem is that our explanation really just took for granted what it was supposed to explain: why *anything at all* gets held up.

A similar circularity plagues the suggestion that the behavior of a person can be explained as the result of the behavior of lots of little people running around inside controlling the full-size person much as if they were controlling a ship.

The explanation is circular because we now need to explain the behavior of these little people. Do we suppose that they have still smaller people running around inside their heads? If so, do these still smaller people have people running round in *their* heads?

Of course, to point out that these explanations are circular is not to prove that there is no elephant or that there are no little people running around inside our heads. But if the only reason for introducing the elephant and those little people in the first place was to explain certain things which, it turns out, they don't explain but just take for granted, then whatever justification we thought we had for introducing them is entirely demolished.

The same, of course, goes for the inner, mental "looking-up" machinery introduced by the inner process model. By showing that this machinery takes for granted what it's supposed to explain, Wittgenstein demolishes the justification we thought we had for introducing it. (Law 2003)

In what, then, does meaning consist? Section 43 of Wittgenstein's *Philosophical Investigations* reads, "For a *large* class of cases—though not for all—in which we employ the word 'meaning,' it can be defined thus: the meaning of a word is its use in the language."

Although it is beyond my abilities to pronounce on this aphorism of the great philosopher, I understand it to say that the meaning of a word coincides with its actual use in the language. It is also my understanding that Wittgenstein is identifying the meaning of language in general with its actual use and, in doing so, is dismissing the idea of "fixed" meaning.

Meaning as an Emergent Phenomenon

Meaning is an emergent phenomenon that manifests itself dependent on, and in response to, a temporary union of relevant conditions. In a sense, meaning may be likened to a spark that is produced when flint and steel come together. Both flint and steel are necessary to the production of a spark, but neither, by itself, is a spark. No matter how carefully we look at the flint or how many pieces we break it into, we will never discover a spark residing anywhere within it. And no matter how closely we look at the steel or how many minute pieces we cut it into, will we never find where the spark comes from. Yet a spark comes forth at the instant when flint and steel meet. Like a spark, meaning emerges when certain conditions are present, integrated, and working together as one. There is no emergence of meaning without conditions, and yet meaning itself cannot be found in any of the individual conditions. On another front, there should be enough heat for a spark to be generated, and the heat is a form of energy caused by the friction occurring when flint and steel are struck together. Similarly, since meaning is not detectable if the conditions are examined singly or independently of each other, we might say that it originates with some kind of energy that is created when the conditions interact.

The Ultimate Source of Meaning

Meaning is often discussed in terms of where it is—or is thought to be—found. Some say it is in language; others say it is in people; still others say it is in the use of language by people. In a sense, they all are correct, depending on the various points they are trying to make.

But in relating meaning to something, perhaps it is more appropriate and cogent (and less divisive) to say that "meaning is *with* that something" than to say "it is *in* it." Meaning is an emergent phenomenon—it emerges with conditions and disappears with the disappearance of conditions. Thus, it should properly be viewed based on conditioned, or dependent, origination.

And still we are faced with the question, where does meaning, in the broadest sense of the word, ultimately originate? My personal belief is that meaning is omnipresent in the universe and, therefore, one with the universe. In a sense, the universe can be viewed as a great accumulation of semantic energy, from which meanings derive or unfold, and I will call this energy "MEANING" (capitalized to distinguish it from the infinity of meanings that derive from it). Meanings that we perceive are the outwardly manifest aspect of MEANING, but MEANING itself cannot be grasped through any concrete form or image. When MEANING manifests itself, it does so only in response to, and dependent on, the temporary union of conditions—including language and intelligent life such as humans. Also, just as the universe is infinite, so, too, is MEANING.

Understood in this way, the relationship between language and human beings can be described in this way:

(42) Language is not meaning itself but is one of many different types of stimulus for meaning to emerge and become active, and the human race is one of many possible forms of intelligent life with unknown capacity that can provide a "place" for the activity of meaning.

The latter part of (42) may sound like too much of a leap, but it is based on my philosophical preference for the panspermic view of life—that the seeds of life are prevalent throughout the universe. In an interview for *Frontline* magazine, Chandra Wickramasinghe, a leading expert on interstellar material and the origins of life, expressed his belief that "the universe must be teeming with intelligent or superintelligent life":

(43) *Frontline:* If life is not unique on the earth, what do you think about the possibilities of the existence of intelligent life in other parts of the universe?

Wickramasinghe: If life on the earth came from space 4,000 million years ago, it continued to arrive even to the present day. I think that this continuing input of bacterial genes contributed immensely to the evolution of life on the earth. The emergence of intelligent creatures like ourselves has been the eventual outcome of these processes. I think the cosmic genes that led to life and eventually intelligence must rain down on every habitable planet in the cosmos. Recent astronomical studies have shown that planet formation might be a commonplace occurrence. Several dozen extra-solar planets have been discovered to date, and this list is growing. Of the 100 billion sun-like stars in our galaxy it is likely now that one per cent or so may have planetary systems like ours. That makes for billions of earth-like planets in our Milky Way alone. The same assemblies of cosmic genes leading to intelligence must then have taken place on a fair fraction of these. So, I believe on this basis that the universe must be teeming with intelligent or super-intelligent life. (*Frontline* 2000)

We will return to the point made in (42) in the final chapter.

3

Emergence of Meaning in the Form of a Story

Language is one of many different types of stimulus for meaning to emerge and become active, and the human mind is a "place" for the activity of meaning. With this in mind, this chapter discusses the phenomenon whereby meaning emerges in the form of a story. Let's begin by returning to the headline from a Japanese *shukanshi* magazine, mentioned in chapter 1:

TWO FEMALE STUDENTS—A HEADACHE FOR PROFESSOR YAMAMOTO

The headline in question had the following syntactic construction:

(44) *[[X wo nayamasu] futarino josei kashu]*
(Here, "X" is used to refer to a Buddhist leader's name.)

X wo nayamasu is an adjective clause modifying the noun phrase *futarino josei kashu*. *Wo* is a particle denoting that the preceding word (X) is the object of the verb *nayamasu*. *Futarino* is a numerical adjective meaning "two." *Josei kashu,* meaning "female singers," is a noun-noun compound and is analyzed as a combination of adjectival *josei* (female) and head noun *kashu* (singers). The noun phrase *futarino josei kashu* is the sense subject of the verb *nayamasu. Kenkyusha's New Japanese-English Dictionary* (Japan's largest and most comprehensive Japanese-English dictionary) gives the following definitions for the verb *nayamasu:* afflict, torment, harass, agonize, torture, gnaw, lacerate, plague, molest, beset, vex, annoy, worry, bother, embarrass, trouble, be troublesome to, persecute, oppress. However, in the case of (44), the meaning of the verb would best be conveyed by the translation "be a headache for," and that of (44) as a whole by the translation "two female singers—a headache for X."

(45) TWO FEMALE SINGERS—A HEADACHE FOR X

Here is a summary of the article's content:

(46) Rumor is that two female celebrity members (the two female singers mentioned in the headline) of X's Buddhist organization are on bad terms. This must be causing a headache for him.

There is no doubt that the audience who read both the headline and the article found the headline totally misleading. The question is *why* the readers experience a discrepancy between their interpretation of the headline and the actual content of the article. What expectations does the headline create in them, and why? In dealing with this question, let's use a slightly modified version of the original headline (47a) and the corresponding article summary (47b).

(47) a. Headline:

Two Female Students—A Headache for Professor Yamamoto

b. Article summary:

Rumor is that two female students in Professor Yamamoto's seminar class are on bad terms. This must be causing a headache for him.

If (47a) is a *shukanshi* magazine headline, what expectations does it set up for us? First, we are influenced by the very fact that it is a *shukanshi* magazine headline. This is because, when a dog bites a man, that is not news, since it happens so often. But if a man bites a dog, that is news. We expect the article to be about something scandalous or shocking. This expectation then gives rise to certain assumptions. For example, is Professor Yamamoto male or female? We can't tell. Yet the headline leads us to infer strongly, or almost presuppose, that the professor is male. Next, in what way are the students a headache for the professor? Although each word in (47a) by itself does not say for certain, the headline as a whole creates a false image of the professor as being involved in a romantic relationship with both students.

The article under the headline is simply about a bad relationship *between* the two students, but our interpretation of the headline is influenced by how each party is introduced—and the magazine's editor is well aware of it. For example, why has the editor chosen "two *female* students" instead of "two students"? Because he knows that just by his choices and arrangements of words, he can manipulate the reader's associations and let the activated associations interact. He knows that the reader constructs a story on the basis of the linguistic stimuli presented in the headline—a story in which the "womanizing" professor is found out by his two student "lovers" and faces their angry reproaches—and he anticipates that the reader will be tempted to buy the magazine for the full story.

Homo Narrans

Meaning that takes the form of a story arises from our contact with "TWO FEMALE STUDENTS—A HEADACHE FOR PROFESSOR YAMAMOTO." Fisher (1987) suggests that human beings are *Homo narrans,* or storytelling creatures. Indeed, it seems that we have a tendency to respond to various stimuli from our environment, including linguistic ones, by "inserting them into a story or narrative." David Herman writes,

> (48) It may very well be that in running away from you
> when you come at me with your fist raised, I do
> so because I have managed to insert your overt
> actions (taking a particular path of motion, raising
> your fist, etc.) into a narrative, by which I impute
> to you motivations and goals and also project the
> likely outcome of your actions should I take no
> countervailing steps. (Herman 2000)

If storytelling is one of the key identifying features of human beings, exploring how stories are constructed will reveal something important about us—about our cognitive processes, our choices of actions, our nature as human beings, and so on. As an example, consider this: I am a Japanese national, and right now I am writing this part of my book late at night in a first-floor apartment in Manhattan, New York City, where I am temporarily staying. Suppose I suddenly hear a voice crying "Fire!" What will I do? I will run out of my apartment building. But what if I hear a shout, "Robber!"? I will stay inside. What would be the underlying reason behind this difference in my choice of actions? It seems that I choose what I do or do not do, based on the different stories I construct reflexively in response to the different linguistic stimuli.

(49) a. Linguistic stimulus: "Fire!"

    b. Story in my mind: "I go outside, look for where the fire is, rest assured for now that there is no danger of the fire spreading as far as my building." Or "I go outside; look for where the fire is; see the danger of my building catching fire; go back to my apartment to get my passport, the flash memory card in which my manuscript is stored, and so on; go to a safe location."

(50) a. Linguistic stimulus: "Robber!"

    b. Story in my mind: "If I go out now, I run into the robber and become the eyewitness. The robber, who has a gun, shoots me."

These stories are the products of my imagination. And yet they are real to me. "Fire" and "robber" are only words, but when these linguistic stimuli are embedded in stories, they become the objects of sharper awareness, and each situation morphs into a synthesis of more vivid experience. It is as if I were running a video in my mind's eye. Also, it is the intuitive, rather than the logical, part of my mind that concocts the stories.

Anyway, if storytelling is one of the key identifying features of human beings, exploring why and how stories are constructed will reveal something about our nature. In the sections that follow, we will pursue these questions in more detail.

Gestalt Principles

We have a tendency to use stories to understand and interpret our world. But what are the factors or principles that underlie our propensity for story-making? In trying to answer the question, I first refer to the knowledge provided by Gestalt psychology, because Gestalt psychology is concerned with how we try to make sense of the stimuli or information we encounter by organizing parts into wholes.

To begin our investigation (and for the sake of introducing some gestalt ideas), suppose there is a symbol that takes the form of "A." If we encounter this in (51), we will most likely take it to be "H."

(51) TAE

But our perception of "A" is subject to change depending on the environment that surrounds the symbol. For example, in (52) we will find it presented as "A."

(52) CAT

The *objective* fact, assuming there is one, is that "A" is not "H" or "A." Nor is it even a linguistic sign (at least for us). It follows, then, that we choose to see it as "H" or as "A."

While psychological processes involved in this kind of perceptual phenomenon can be explained from various viewpoints, here I want to focus on a tendency of the human mind:

(53) The mind has a natural tendency to relate and unite things that are located close together, in an effort to make the string or sequence meaningful.

As Chandler (1997) rightly points out, "We seem as a species to be driven by a desire to make meanings... We are, above all,

Homo significans—meaning-makers… Faced even by 'meaning-less' patterns the mind restlessly strives to make them meaning-ful."

The tendency stated in (53) may be explained in part using Gestalt theory. The "principle of contiguity (or proximity)" in the theory tells us that things that are closer together are perceived as belonging together and, often, as forming a coherent entity. Look at the following example from Chandler (1997):

(54)

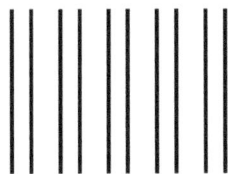

In the figure, we tend to perceive five pairs of lines because they are "close together with fairly broad gaps between them." Regarding why we are "less likely to group together the lines which are further apart," Chandler assumes that it is "perhaps partly because this would leave lonely lines on each side of the image, but also … because we seem to have a predisposition to associate things which are close together." (The first factor that he mentions seems to me very important and powerful. We will come back to this point later.) Based on this principle, we could say that since "T," "A," and "E" (or "C," "A," and "T") are placed together, they are perceived as interrelated in a coherent way.

Another important principle in Gestalt psychology is that of "good continuation." Speaking in broad generalizations, the principle predicts a preference for a smooth and uncomplicated stream of information. When "TAE" is perceived exactly as it is, the irregular and discontinuous aspect of the sequence becomes conspicuous, and we undergo abrupt perceptual transitions—in this case, from an alphabetic letter ("T") to a nonlinguistic symbol (ʌ) and back to an alphabetic letter ("E"). This perceptual experience causes an uncomfortable feeling in us. So the phenomenon of seeing "ʌ" as "H" can be explained in terms of the good-continuation principle. Since we prefer to see smooth continuity in "TʌE," we perceptually modify the sequence and create a percept that meets our expectation, namely, "THE."

Another Gestalt principle that would be relevant in the present context is the "principle of closure."

(55)) {) {) {) {

Here we tend to see three sets of ( ) rather than four sets of) (. This illustrates the principle of closure, which states, "Of several geometrically possible perceptual organizations, the one that produces a 'closed' rather than an 'open' figure will be perceived."

This principle seems to override the contiguity, or proximity, principle. Again citing Chandler,

(56) *Closure* is a … principle of perceptual organization: *interpretations which produce 'closed' rather than 'open' figures are favoured.*

Here we tend to see three broken rectangles (and a lonely shape on the far left) rather than three 'girder'

profiles (and a lonely shape on the right). In this case the principle of closure cuts across the principle of proximity, since if we remove the bracket shapes, we [have] an image [that illustrates] proximity.

(Chandler 1997)

I presume that our preference for a closed configuration is associated with our preference for a configuration that has no remainder. Speaking simplistically, we tend to prefer (57a) to (57b) because the former is closed and the latter open, and we prefer (57a) to (57c) because the former has no remainder, whereas the latter does—in this case, [on the far right.

(57) a. [ ]
   b.] [
   c. [ ] [

In some respects, (57c) is psychologically uncomfortable, because it leaves us with a sense of "noncompletion" or "partial completion" (as if we had left it unfinished).

Now, the closure principle further recognizes that we tend to see "complete" figures even when part of the information is missing. To illustrate this, look at (58):

(58)

On the left, for example, we tend to see a "closed" and therefore "complete" circle, even though what is actually drawn is three curved lines close to one another. This phenomenon shows that the human mind *is able* and *prefers* to see perceived incomplete patterns as closed and complete.

What implications does the principle of closure have for the analysis of "T⅄E" and "C⅄T"? First of all, we are uncomfortable with something that is unfamiliar, ambiguous, uncertain, or incomplete, because it is "open" to interpretation rather than being fixed or "closed." "⅄" is a symbol that gives us such an undesirable feeling, and naturally we want to alleviate this uncomfortable state. How? We try to do so by associating it with something familiar, most likely with a linguistic sign. In other words, we are "psychologically ready" to see it as "H" or "A."

Second, we tend not only to perceive elements that are close together as forming a group, but also to see the group as a unified whole or a single structure rather than merely the sum of its parts. If we apply this observation to "T⅄E" and "C⅄T," it could be said that we are inclined to assume them to be closed and complete semantic units, or "semantic gestalts."

Third, the closure principle suggests that the whole is primary and governs the parts. In our cognitive process of interpreting "T⅄E" and "C⅄T," it seems that the formation of a mental representation of the whole takes priority and that we adjust the interpretation of the parts to match the representation.

Finally, our interpretation of "T⅄E" and "C⅄T" is an active mental process in that it involves creating representations that are not mere reproductions of these stimuli. This appears to be analogous to the phenomenon in which we construct a percept of a complete circle from a circle-with-gaps stimulus. It can be viewed as a phenomenon in which we "finish" the broken circle or "repair" it by welding. Similarly, we mentally transform the deformed "/\" into familiar and meaningful linguistic signs. Further, we interpret "T/\E" and "C/\T" as "THE" and "CAT" respectively, not as "TAE" and "CHT." Simply identifying "/\" as a linguistic sign does not bring us a sense of "closure" or "completeness." As we noted, this is because we are always looking for meaning, but also note that meaning-seekers are often meaning-makers. We are not content or comfortable with recognizing the stimuli as arbitrary sequences of alphabetic letters, and therefore, our minds actively create meaning by integrating the signs into semantic gestalts. In this sense, "THE" and "CAT" are the products of our mental activity.

The above are just a few of the better-known gestalt principles—there are many others. But even these alone contain significant and helpful suggestions for understanding our ability, tendency, and motivation to develop a story based on limited input information. For example, consider the following, from Lebedev (2006):

(59) "Hi baby, may I ask you   "I'm gonna pummel
        for a dance?   your ass!"

What we objectively perceive with our eyes is an image of a male, a female, and another male, standing in that order in a row, with the female closer to the male on the right. But our mental activity does not stop at this basic visual cognition. If I introspect on what is going on in my mind, I find myself inventing expository sentences that explain or interpret the relationships between the "characters" in (59). The sentences go like this:

(60) The picture represents a relationship involving three people. Since one of them is female and the other two are male, something more than friendship is implied. The woman and the man on the right are together romantically. The man on the left liked the woman but was rejected.

The above can be analyzed as follows:

(61) a. The woman and the man on the right in (59) are grouped together according to the principle of proximity, and the physical proximity is interpreted as indicating an intimacy in their relationship.

b. The human figures in (59) are at uneven distances from each other, and we experience a sense of discontinuity between the man on the left and the woman. In (60), this visually experienced discontinuity is interpreted as corresponding to the lack of smoothness, or the rift, in human relations between the two.

c. The figure (59) is composed of a lone male figure and a pair consisting of a male and a female figure and therefore, viewed in its entirety, does not fulfill the quality of a gestalt. In other words, as far as visual perception is concerned, our experience of it is not really integrated. The mental activity described in (60) seems to be motivated toward providing a unified meaning to (59)—that is, my mind is trying to integrate the three people into a semantic gestalt by incorporating them into a love triangle story.

Inference

As human beings, we are driven by a desire to make meanings, and our propensity for story-making is closely linked to this desire. The important question in our context, then, is, how is meaning *made*? This section pays particular attention to the role of "inference" in the process of meaning-making.

As a starting point, let's take the opening scene of the film *Working Girl*.

(62) Opening Scene:

The scene begins with a close-up of the face of the Statue of Liberty. Then the camera, pulling back from it, circles around until we see the back of the statue, and a ferry crossing New York Bay behind it. From the camera angle and the wake behind the boat, we can deduce that the ferry is heading from Staten Island toward Manhattan. At this point, the introduction part of the theme song "Let the River Run" finishes, and the song itself begins:

"Let the river run,
Let all the dreamers

Wake the nation,

Come, the New Jerusalem…"

Then the camera rotates farther to the right until we see the skyline of Manhattan, where the boat is heading. It's an early morning scene. The camera then zooms in on the ferry, on whose side the words "Staten Island Ferry CITY OF NEW YORK" are painted. Here we understand that it is a commuter ferry transporting "working people" from Staten Island to Manhattan. The camera pans through the ferry's crowded interior, focusing on two women on a bench seat. Both women have "big" hair. One of the women is presenting a cupcake with three lit candles on it to the other and singing, "…Te-ess, happy birthday to you." At that point, Tess laughs and blows out the candles. Her friend then removes the candles and asks her if she made a wish. To this she replies, "Yeah," and stares off dreamily at the skyline.

The ferry arrives at the harbor; then a crowd of people from the ferry are seen flowing out onto a walkway. Then the scene cuts to show a sidewalk, where a crowd of people are walking in the same direction. In the middle of this scene, the camera follows the two women shown earlier in the ferry. As they are walking toward their office building, they have the following conversation:

Tess: No lunch. I got speech class.

Cyn: What do you need speech class for? You talk fine. All right. I'll pick you up at five. We'll ride back together.

> *Tess:* I can't. I got Emerging Markets Seminar at five thirty.
>
> *Cyn:* Jeez, it's your birthday. Can't they emerge without you just this once?
>
> *Tess:* What time is my surprise party?
>
> *Cyn:* What?
>
> *Tess:* Come on.
>
> *Cyn:* Oh, I'm supposed to take you to drinks, have you home at seven.
>
> *Tess:* Okay, I'll cut out early and be home at seven fifteen, okay?
>
> *Cyn:* All right.
>
> *Tess:* Thank you very much.

At the end of the conversation, we see them playfully trying to shove each other off the curb. Then we see them enter a busy office lobby and walk across the lobby toward the elevator. The scene then changes to the interior of a busy open-plan office as Tess walks toward her desk.

After watching this scene, I found myself having formed certain expectations about how the story would unfold, which in turn prompted me to ask myself why and how I had generated those expectations. Simply stated, I assumed from this scene that the theme of the movie is the American dream, and my expectations were based on this assumption. In other words, I derived a meaning (a thematic meaning) from the scene. The next question, then, is, why this assumption? My introspection tells me that I was reacting to the scene by asking questions in my mind, by engaging in an inner dialogue with the input stimuli from the scene, consciously and subconsciously.

(63) a. The Statue of Liberty and the Manhattan skyline—what ideas or associations do they inspire?

b. The two women (Tess and Cyn) talking in the ferry—what words and ideas should I use to describe them?

c. The woman called Tess must be the main character. What is her age? Her income? Marital status? Educational background? Social class?

d. The interior shot of the ferry, where Cyn asks Tess if she made a wish and Tess replies, "Yeah," and stares off dreamily at the skyline, is evocative. Although the line "Yeah" is just one short utterance, it is highly expressive because of the character's intonation, tone of voice, and facial expression and the way she "stares off dreamily at the skyline." What are the character's inner thoughts? Her emotions?

e. Let's look again at the following dialogue between Tess and Cyn:

Tess: No lunch. I got speech class.

Cyn: What do you need speech class for? You talk fine. All right. I'll pick you up at five. We'll ride back together.

Tess: I can't. I got Emerging Markets Seminar at five thirty.

Cyn: Jeez, it's your birthday. Can't they emerge without you just this once?

What does this conversation reveal about Tess? What makes her work so hard? What wish did she make when she blew out the candles?

f. Why did the director choose the song "Let the River Run" to start the movie?

g. What does the director want to convey in this opening scene?

In the process of trying to answer these questions, the story had already begun in my mind: a story about a hardworking (but struggling) woman pursuing (and ultimately realizing) the American dream. If you watch the whole film, you will actually see that the theme of the film is precisely this.

Frederic and Mary Ann Brussat, in their review of *Working Girl*, write,

(64) "If you can dream it," said Walt Disney, "you can do it." That's the theme of *Working Girl*. Tess McGill is a hard-working secretary who lives in Staten Island. After several bad experiences with male chauvinist bosses who don't take her aspirations for self-improvement very seriously, she lands a secretarial position with Katharine Parker, a driven executive in the mergers and acquisitions division of a top brokerage firm.

Impressed with her new employee's skills and ambition, Katharine listens carefully when Tess explains her idea for how Trask Industries can ward off a takeover bid by purchasing radio stations. Later, when Katharine is injured in a ski accident, Tess learns that her boss has stolen her idea and set it in motion with Jack Trainer, an investment banker. Realizing that it is now or never for her dream of corporate advancement, Tess seizes the moment and decides to handle the deal herself. (Frederic Brussat and Mary Ann Brussat 1988)

In other words, while watching the three-and-a-half-minute opening scene of the film, I began to "co-construct the story" with the director. I was not just a passive recipient of the scene, but an active participant in the production of meaning.

Now, I was co-constructing the story based on the theme of the film, but what guided me to the awareness of the theme? The film does not begin, for example, with a narrator's voice-over stating that the theme is the American dream. What the director does is *hint* about it. The scene itself does not provide any answers directly to the questions mentioned in (63), but it invited me to *infer* them. And so I did, though the granularity of inference varied depending on the kinds of questions. Wuming Zhao explains how the Statue of Liberty (the symbol of freedom and opportunity) is used in the scene:

(65) The opening scene of Working Girl is a 360° aerial shot of the Statue of Liberty. When the camera, leading all the audience, soars around in the morning light, from a close-up of the goddess's confident and inspiring face to a long shot of the entire Statue [of Liberty] with her right arm tirelessly holding up the torch lit with hope and the American spirit, the boundless water, land and sky all around her, it not only sets forth the tone for the movie—a liberation story of a working girl in the central business jungle of New York—but also invites the audience into a

symbolic and fantasy world where one is supposed to be able to enjoy the freedom of a flying bird, and all the possibilities and opportunities such freedom implies. (Zhao 1996)

Likewise, I sought explanations of the scene in my mind, making inferences on the basis of what I saw, what I heard, and what the characters said to each other.

As we observed above, inferences play an important role in the process of meaning-making, and they occur in all kinds of meaning-making acts. Here, however, we will focus mainly on inferences in natural language information processing.

Linguistic information processing almost always involves some form of inference, because in ordinary language use, people do not make everything explicit. Look at the following example:

(66) A baseball fan is glued to the tube during the course of a historic World Series between the Red Sox and the Cubs. The teams are tied at three games apiece. His wife is losing patience with him and, not knowing that the Series is best of seven, wants to know how much more baseball she'll have to put up with. He assures her, "They'll play only one more game." Since they will meet again in interleague play the following season, what he said was not really true, but that's not what he meant. (Bach 2001)

Now, the baseball fan could have made fully explicit what he was trying to convey, by saying, "The Red Sox and the Cubs will play only one more game in the current World Series." But as Bach points out, "…we don't have to…since ordinarily we can rely on our audience's ability to figure out the intended qualification."

In our use of language, we tend to put a premium on efficiency, trying to minimize our effort. Bach explains:

(67) We commonly speak loosely, by omitting words that could have made what we meant more explicit, and we let our audience fill in the gaps. Language works far more efficiently when we do that. Literalism can have its virtues, like when we're drawing up a contract or programming a computer, but we generally opt for efficiency over explicitness. In most conversation, though, spelling things out is not only unnecessary, it just slows things down. (Bach 2001)

Indeed, human language is "lazy" in a sense, or it is a "rough" tool of communication. And therefore, understanding human language almost always requires inference on the part of the hearer/reader. By inference, I mean "any piece of information that is not explicitly said or written" (McKoon and Ratcliff 1992) and "any assertion which the hearer/reader comes to believe to be true as a result of hearing/reading something which is said/written explicitly" (Norvig 1987).

Asher and Lascarides illustrate this point well:

(68) People don't make explicit many aspects of what we take to be part of the discourse's meaning ... Instead, interpreters infer, and are expected to infer, information over and above what's derivable from the meaning of the individual words and syntax. While this happens even when constructing the meaning of a clause, it is pervasive when constructing the

meaning of a multi-sentence discourse. Consider the simple text (1ab), for example:

(1) a. John arrived in Edinburgh by train.

  b. Max met him at the station.

    A competent language user infers that *the station* is the station where John's train arrived (and hence it's in Edinburgh) and John's arrival happened before his meeting with Max. Without these inferences, it becomes difficult to understand which station is being talked about or indeed why the speaker juxtaposed the sentences. (Asher and Lascarides 2003)

Here are some more examples, with the Q and A taking place in the hearer's/reader's mind:

(69) John bought a car. The engine has 280 horsepower.

  Q: Why did the speaker/writer juxtapose these two sentences? How do the sentences relate semantically? Why does "engine," which is not mentioned before, have the definite article "the" in front of it?

  A: Cars have engines. "The engine" refers to the engine of the car John bought.

(70) "The man drove past our house in a car. The exhaust fumes were terrible" (Hawkins 1978).

  Q: Why the definite description "*the* exhaust fumes"?

  A: Cars have engines. "The man *drove* past our house in a car" means that the engine of the car he was driving was in operation. When a car engine is in operation, the car emits exhaust fumes (from burning a hydrocarbon fuel). "The exhaust fumes" refers to the exhaust fumes emitted from the man's car.

(71) "Ellen," he said, picking up her name from when he had whispered it years ago, "there's just one thing."

"What?"

"I'm getting married in a couple of months."

"Oh." That changed the complexion of everything. "Why didn't you tell me first?"...

"Is she Irish?" she asked at length, because he'd keep up the silence for the whole evening.

"No, she's American." (O'Brien 1980)

Q: To whom does the pronoun "she" in Ellen's "Is she Irish?" refer?

A: Ellen's interlocutor says, "I'm getting married." Since it takes two to get married, "she" is the person he is getting married to.

(72) John was lost. He pulled over to a farmer standing by the side of the road. He asked him where he was.

Q: To whom does each of the three pronouns in the last sentence refer?

A: The first sentence says, "John was lost." When you get lost, you want to know where you are. The second sentence, "He pulled over to a farmer standing by the side of the road," means that John went near the farmer. When you go near someone standing by the side of the road, you do so because you want something from him or her. What John wanted was to know where he was. Also, when you want to know what you don't know, you ask someone who, you think, will have the answer. The farmer standing by the roadside is most likely to be a local resident and know the area well. Therefore, in the last sentence, the first pronoun, *he,* refers to John, the second pronoun, *him,* refers to the farmer, and the third pronoun, *he,* refers to John (Norvig (1987).

(73) Ax murder

Q: What is the underlying semantic relation between "ax" and "murder"?

A: Since murder is an act of killing another human being intentionally, it involves a killer, a victim, and a (set of) motive(s). Also, it is often the case that when someone kills someone else, he or she uses some kind of weapon. An ax is a tool for cutting trees, chopping wood, and so on. But at the same time, it is possible that someone might use an ax as a murder weapon. Therefore, "ax murder" refers to a murder, using an ax as a weapon.

(74) locked-room murder

Q: What is the underlying semantic relation between "locked-room" and "murder"?

A: Murder is an act. An act involves somebody doing something (often *to* someone or something). Murder is also an event. Both actions and events take place in space and time. In (74), "locked-room" and "murder" are juxtaposed, and so they must have something to do with each other. A room cannot be either a killer or a killed victim in the action or event of murder. Locked-room murder is most likely a murder *in* a locked room.

Quite often, inference-making happens unconsciously, and we are unaware of doing it. In connection with this, I will share an episode. My Canadian friend Linda, who was reading a newspaper near me, suddenly let out a gasp of mixed surprise and indignation. I wondered what it was that surprised and infuriated her. The story was about Jeffrey Dahmer:

(75) **Dahmer: "I Know Society Will Never Forgive Me"**

MILWAUKEE (AP)—Serial killer Jeffrey Dahmer was sentenced to life in prison Monday after some relatives of his 15 victims called him a devil and Dahmer told the judge, "I know society will never be able to forgive me."

Dahmer was stone-faced and spoke in a low monotone as he described his crimes not as acts of hate but the work of a sick man.

"I take all the blame for what I did," he said.

Moments before, nine relatives of Dahmer's victims, many wearing picture pins of their loved ones, described the pain they have suffered because he killed, butchered and had sex with the corpses of their family members.

The hysterical sister of victim Errol Lindsey shouted "Satan!" at Dahmer and screamed, "Jeffrey, I hate you!!" as she lunged toward him, shaking her fist and shouting obscenities. Guards restrained her and she was led away.

A jury decided Saturday that Dahmer, 31, was sane when he killed 15 young men and boys he lured to his home. Dahmer pleaded guilty but insane. (*Asahi Evening News* 1992)

Dahmer's crimes described in the story are heinous enough to shock and offend any reader tremendously. But what triggered Linda's surprise and indignation was the paragraph that immediately followed. (See below.) More specifically, it was the words "the former chocolate factory worker" in the first sentence of the paragraph:

The former chocolate factory worker confessed to 17 slayings since 1978 after his arrest last July. He is to stand trial in an Ohio killing, and wasn't charged in one Milwaukee death because of lack of evidence. (*Asahi Evening News* 1992)

"Why are you so surprised and upset about it?" I asked her, and although her exact answer has escaped my memory now, I do remember that she mentioned *Charlie and the Chocolate Factory*, a classic children's book about a boy named Charlie who goes to a fantasyland of chocolate. Perhaps…

(76) a. While reading the story, she was making vague inferences at an unconscious level about the serial killer's likely background.

　　b. On the other hand, she also had developed unconscious images and inferences about chocolate factory workers that did not fit well with what "the former chocolate factory worker" had done to the "young men and boys," especially to the boys.

Hence her surprise and indignation.

It would not be an overstatement to say that almost every interaction with language is an opportunity to make inferences of some kind. Since early childhood, we have been "groomed" to make inferences about linguistic stimuli (actually, about *all* the stimuli we encounter in our world). To put it another way, language serves as an inference trigger, and again, language is one of many different types of stimuli for meaning to emerge and become active, and the human mind is a "place" for the activity of meaning.

Human beings, who are driven by a desire to make meanings, are also an inference-making species. And the fact that human beings are *Homo narrans*, or storytelling creatures, could be understood as a natural consequence of their being inference-making creatures.

What, then, is a story, or narrative? (We can use "story" and "narrative" interchangeably in this discussion.) Here are the relevant results from a 2006 Internet search, with the search queries "define: story" and "define: narrative," and the definition (77c) by Manfred Jahn.

> (77) a. *story:* a message that tells the particulars of an act or occurrence or course of events; a piece of fiction that narrates a chain of related events
>
> b. *narrative:* a message that tells the particulars of an act or occurrence or course of events

c. "A story is a sequence of events which involves *characters*" (Jahn 2005).

Based on these definitions, is (78) a story?

(78) A hiker bought a pair of boots from a cobbler.

Yes and no. First, why no? Because, although the sentence describes an act of buying, it doesn't seem to tell the "particulars" of the act. Also, it narrates an event (of buying) but not "a chain of related events" or "a sequence of events."

And why yes? Because, upon encountering (78), we unconsciously make a series of inferences:

(79) a. The hiker wanted shoes.

b. The hiker went to a cobbler.

c. The hiker found a pair of boots in the cobbler's store.

d. The hiker bought the boots.

e. The hiker now owns the boots that previously belonged to the cobbler.

f. The cobbler now has some money that previously belonged to the hiker.

g. The hiker will probably use the boots in his avocation rather than, say, give them as a gift to his sister. (See also Norvig 1987.)

We can acknowledge that (79) has a storylike structure. In other words, (78) may not be a story by outward appearances, but in the unconscious mind of the hearer/reader, its meaning emerges in a storylike form. Seen in that light, (78) serves as a story trigger, and therefore, it potentially possesses "storyness."

Now let us consider a more rigorous definition of story/narrative. Noël Carroll, in his paper "On the Narrative Connection" (2001), tries to make clear what types of discourses count as a narrative, using the notion of narrative connection. He makes a distinction between "chronicles," "annals," and "narratives." Velleman gives an excellent analysis and commentary on Carroll's work:

(80) Carroll distinguishes among three modes of discourse for recounting events: *annals,* which represent events as temporally ordered; *chronicles,* which represent temporally ordered events pertaining to a single subject; and *narrative,* which requires some additional connection among the events:

> If I say, "I woke up; later I dressed; still later I went to class," I suspect that most people would agree that this falls short of a full-fledged narrative, although the events cited might be turned into ingredients of a narrative. But why isn't it a narrative properly so called? To put it vaguely— because the connection among the events alluded to by it is not tight enough. [119–20]

> The connection that is "tight enough" to transform a chronicle into a narrative, according to Carroll, is the connection between causes and the effects for which they were, in the circumstances, necessary (though perhaps not sufficient). Carroll illustrates the need for such "narrative connections" by means of the following example:

> Consider this putative narrative: "Aristarchus hypothesized the heliocentric theory thereby

anticipating Copernicus' discovery by many centuries."... If there is no line of influence stretching from Aristarchus' discovery to Copernicus', I, at least, find it strained to think that this is narrative. It is an interesting series of events. Indeed, mention of the second event in this series retrospectively reveals something of the significance of the earlier event, and... retrospective significance is a frequently occurring feature of narrative. However, where the events bear no sort of causal relation to each other, they seem more of the order of coincidence than of narrative.... [125]

Retrospective significance, though a typically recurring and explicable feature of narrative should not be mistaken as the mark of narrative. For the temporally ordered discourse "Aristarchus hypothesized the heliocentric system and then centuries later Copernicus discovered it again" affords the apprehension of retrospective significance—it indicates the point of mentioning Aristarchus' discovery in light of Copernicus'—but it is not, as I have argued, a narrative proper inasmuch as it lacks a narrative connection." [127]

In Carroll's terminology, the discoveries of Aristarchus and Copernicus are ingredients for a chronicle but not a narrative, because they are successive events pertaining to a common topic but are causally unrelated... Carroll goes on to suggest that the causal content of a narrative underlies its explanatory potential:

Perhaps a related consideration in favor of my view of narrative is that narrative is a common form of explanation. In ordinary speech, we use narratives to explain how things happened and why certain standing conditions were important. Narrative is capable of performing this role because it tracks causal networks... Thus, insofar as what we call narratives are explanatory, it seems advisable to regard narrative properly so called as connected to causation and not merely temporal succession. [128] (Velleman 2002)

Worth also explains Carroll's point using E. M. Forster's (1927) often cited example:

(81) If the elements in a narrative connection bear no sort of causal relation to each other, then they can seem to be more of an order of coincidence than of a narrative. For example,

   D: the king died and then the queen died.

   E: the king died and then the queen died, of grief.

   D is merely a chronicle because there is no causal or underdetermined identifiable underlying cause or explanation from the first event to the second event. It is not clear to a reader, nor can it really be discerned, what the relationship is between the two events although they seem to have a unified subject and there is an implied temporal order. E, on the other hand, is a narrative because the relationship between the two (unified, temporally ordered) events is made clear. (Worth 2005)

Now, with Carroll's definition in mind, we will look at the relationship between narrative and inference:

(82) Mary got pregnant and she got married.

Is this a narrative or not? Instead of answering the question with a simple yes or no, I prefer to waffle yet again and say that it is *potentially* a narrative, because "narrative," like meaning, is an emergent phenomenon. It emerges with conditions and disappears with the disappearance of conditions. It should be viewed based on conditioned origination or dependent origination. Language is not, in itself, narrative, but it is a *stimulus* for narrative to emerge, and human mind is a *place* for narrative to emerge. Narrative arises as a result of the *interplay* of those conditions (i.e., language and human mind). For example, compare (83) and (84):

(83) Mary got infected and she got married.

(84) Mary got infected and she went to the hospital (Bach 2002).

Although the two sentences have the same coordinate structure, (83) is less likely to serve as a stimulus for narrative to emerge, because the hearer's/reader's mind finds it difficult to see the reason why the two conjuncts are coordinated. On the other hand, like (82), (84) is more likely to serve as a narrative trigger. We will come back to this point later.

There could also be a case where the other condition—that is, hearer/reader—does not respond to a narrative trigger. Consider the following example from Blamires:

(85) *Speech Therapist:* It says here that archaeologists have discovered a skull of a 10-year-old boy in Italy, which they think might be that of Christopher Columbus. Why do you think that might be wrong?

 Child: I don't know.

Speech Therapist: What did Christopher Columbus do?

Child: He discovered America in 1642.

Speech Therapist: How old was he when he did that? He must have been grown up.

Child: He was 32.

Speech Therapist: He must have died when he was quite old then.

Child: When he was 55.

Speech Therapist: So could the skull of the boy have been Christopher Columbus's?

Child: I'm not sure.

The child knows a lot of facts about Christopher Columbus but he cannot link them to common understanding of death and skeletons. Our bodies contain skeletons, which grow with us, and we only have one. If the child's skull was Christopher Columbus's, he would have had to die when he was a child. (Blamires 1999)

If a reader of (82), like the child in the dialogue, misses the semantic connection between "pregnancy" and "marriage," no narrative will emerge in that reader's mind. But what about (86)?

(86) Mary got pregnant and *then* she got married, *because of her pregnancy.*

In (86), the temporal sequence and consequence relations between Mary's pregnancy and her marriage are given in explicit language. And yet, (86) would still not be a narrative for that reader, because the reader's understanding of the causal relationship is based only on knowledge about language. I presume that (86) is to that reader as (87) is to me.

(87) Mary got infected and then she got married *because of her infection.*

If someone asks me why Mary got married, I can answer, "Because she got infected," based on my knowledge of the English language, but (87) is not a narrative for me (at least, not a "good" one).

The above observation suggests that it is difficult to decide what is or is not a narrative solely on the basis of linguistic features. Narrative is not statically fixed in linguistic code. It is something that emerges dynamically when language and the human mind work together.

Let's return to (82):

(82) Mary got pregnant and she got married.

Logically, (82) can be a case in which the second conjunct is a "pure addition" to the first (Quirk et al. 1985), and there is no temporal or causal relationship between the two events described in the sentence. However, we almost automatically understand it to mean (82').

(82') Mary got pregnant and *then* she got married.

In our mind, the event described in the second conjunct of (82) is *chronologically sequent* to the event in the first conjunct. But this temporal sequence is cancelable, without contradiction, by adding "not (necessarily) in that order": "Mary got pregnant and she got married, *but not (necessarily) in that order*" (Grice 1975, 1989). In other words, the sequence is not determined by the literal meaning of (82), but rather we *infer* it. We infer that order of mention corresponds to order of events, unless the speaker/writer indicates otherwise.

Literally speaking, (82') is a chronicle but not a narrative. It is not a narrative, for the same reason that "the king died and then the queen died" is not a narrative—until Mary's pregnancy and her marriage are causally related. And the mind actually relates the two events causally; that is, we usually automatically understand (82') to mean

(82") Mary got pregnant and *then, because of her pregnancy,* she got married.

The same holds true for (84). When we read it, we intuitively understand it to mean that Mary got infected and *then, because of her infection,* went to the hospital (Bach 2002). But since the italicized words are not part of (82), we *infer* the causal relationship that is not explicitly stated in (82). Thus, (82) becomes a narrative through our inference.

From a strictly literal standpoint, (82) is not, by itself, a narrative. Rather, it potentially possesses "narrativity" and serves as a narrative trigger. Through inference, the hearer/reader gives a cause for Mary's act of getting married—the narrative meaning implicit in (82) is made explicit through inference—though we are unaware of it because of the automaticity of our inference process.

In a sense, the two events described in (82) could be likened to "a shot of a coffin followed by the face of an old woman weeping" in (88):

(88) In the case of the moving images of television and cinema, the juxtaposition of images one after another

often invites the viewer to infer some connection between them and this confers narrative coherence. For instance if a shot of a coffin is followed by the face of an old woman weeping we assume that she is lamenting the death of whoever is in the coffin. (Central Queensland University 2001)

When we see the sequence of camera shots in this way, we are actively participating in the production of meaning by adding narration to the sequence in our mind. We are co-constructing a narrative that explains the scene. And the same phenomenon is occurring when we read (82). The fact that we are an inference-making species provides a platform to explain the phenomenon whereby meaning emerges in the form of a story or narrative.

Frame

This section discusses the relationship between narrative meaning and the concept of "frame." Narrative meaning, in its broadest sense, is about connections. It is something that combines parts into a coherent and understandable whole. Narrative meaning often owes its emergence to *frame,* which serves as an integrative power, a glue that holds the parts together.

First of all, what is a frame? According to George Lakoff,

(89) A frame is a conceptual structure used in thinking. The word *elephant* evokes a frame with an image of an elephant and certain knowledge: an elephant is a large animal (a mammal) with large floppy ears, a trunk that functions like both a nose and a hand, large stump-like legs, and so on. (Lakoff 2004a)

Using this explanation, we can say,

(90) a. A frame has a *structure* representing a concept.

    b. A frame is something that is *evoked* by some kind of stimulus—for example, by language.

    c. A frame consists of an image and certain *knowledge* of the stimulus that triggers the frame. The knowledge seems to be commonsense knowledge.

Frame, then, is a concept similar to that of "schema." Schemas (or schemata) are cognitive structures or knowledge structures in long-term memory that we use to make sense of things. They are a mental framework or "template" derived from prior experience and knowledge and are used to interpret and organize incoming information. And they are activated by stimuli from our environment, including linguistic ones.

Consider the following example again (from section 4 of this chapter):

(91) Ax murder

    Q: What is the underlying semantic relation between "ax" and "murder"?

    A: Since murder is an act of killing another human being intentionally, it involves a killer, a victim, and motive(s). Also, it is often the case that when someone kills someone else, the killer uses some kind of weapon. Ax is a tool for cutting trees, chopping wood, and so on. But at the same time, it is possible that someone might use an ax as a murder weapon. Therefore, "ax murder" refers to a murder using an ax as a weapon.

Note that when we encounter a noun-noun compound such as "ax murder," we make a connection between the nouns—a connection that is not explicit in the expression—using our schematic knowledge activated by the linguistic input(s) or cue(s). Schemas serve as the integrative power, or glue, that holds together the parts of the linguistic input. Consider John Bransford and Marcia Johnson's example below:

(92) The procedure is actually quite simple. First you arrange things into different groups. Of course, one pile may be sufficient depending on how much there is to do. If you have to go somewhere else due to lack of facilities that is the next step, otherwise you are pretty well set. It is important not to overdo things. That is, it is better to do too few things at once than too many. In the short run this may not seem important but complications can easily arise. A mistake can be expensive as well. At first the whole procedure will seem complicated. Soon, however, it will become just another facet of life. It is difficult to foresee any end to the necessity for this task in the immediate future, but then one never can tell. After the procedure is completed one arranges the material into different groups again. Then they can be put into their appropriate places. Eventually they will be used once more and the whole cycle will then have to be repeated. However, that is part of life. (Bransford and Johnson 1972)

We find it difficult to comprehend this passage, but the difficulty is not in understanding the individual sentences. The problem is that those "parts" seem incoherent with each other, and the passage as a whole does not seem to make much sense. In other words, our understanding of the passage cannot come solely from understanding its component parts. Now, if we are told that the passage is entitled "Washing Clothes," the picture becomes much clearer. This is because the activation of the schema for washing clothes helps us integrate the parts into a meaningful whole. For example, as Smith and Swinney point out, we

> ...would use defaults (such as that clothes are separated into piles and that these piles are inserted into washing and drying machines) to instantiate "procedure" with "the process of washing clothes," "things" with "clothes," "pile" with "pile of clothes," and "facilities" with "washing and drying machines." We would also use the *washing clothes* schema to determine the relations between the various propositions, such as that the procedure referred to in the first sentence includes the operations described in successive sentences. (Smith and Swinney 1992)

Frames and schemas are basically the same in that they are part of the cognitive architecture that guides our processing of information and are triggered by various stimuli from our environment, including linguistic ones. However, the concept of frame as introduced by Lakoff seems to be more pertinent to the phenomenon whereby meaning emerges in the form of a story. Here is Chua's (2006) explanation:

(93) WHAT IS FRAMING?

> The term "framing" comes from cognitive science, which defines a frame as a conceptual structure involved with thinking. To paraphrase an example used by the framing expert George Lakoff, saying

the word "elephant" evokes the elephant frame, which is associated with the terms "animal," "big," "grey," "floppy ears," etc. The elephant frame might be depicted schematically as follows:

Animal

Big

Elephant

Grey

Floppy ears

The above is a simplified diagram, as "animal," "big," "grey," and "floppy ears" each have secondary associations of their own.

Framing can be thought of as telling a story about the world. The elephant frame tells a story about a big, grey animal with floppy ears called "elephant." More broadly, there is a popular American cultural narrative in which hard working people who pull themselves up by their bootstraps will succeed in life. This "hard work equals success" frame is an important way in which many Americans think about the world. Frames are fundamentally about our relationship to the world and how we view it.

WHY IS FRAMING IMPORTANT?

The essence of social change is changing perceptions, which itself is the territory of framing. George Lakoff illustrates the power of framing to effect social change by analyzing the term "tax relief," which is an often-used term used to refer to cutting taxes. To quote Lakoff [2004a]:

"The word *relief* evokes a frame in which there is a blameless Afflicted Person who we identify with and who has some Affliction, some pain or harm that is imposed by some external Cause-of-pain. Relief is the taking away of the pain or harm, and it is brought about by some Reliever-of-pain.

The Relief frame is an instance of a more general Rescue scenario, in which there is a Hero (The Reliever-of-pain), a Victim (the Afflicted), a Crime (the Affliction), a Villain (the Cause-of-affliction), and a Rescue (the Pain Relief). The Hero is inherently good, the Villain is evil, and the Victim after the Rescue owes gratitude to the Hero.

The term *tax relief* evokes all of this and more. Taxes, in this phrase, are the Affliction (the Crime), proponents of taxes are the Causes-of-Affliction (the Villains), the taxpayer is the Afflicted Victim, and the proponents of 'tax relief' are the Heroes who deserve the taxpayers' gratitude." (Chua 2006)

We have a frame for an object, person, action, event, and so on. For example, Schank and Abelson's going-to-a-restaurant frame (event frame) would evoke a story in our mind that has the following characteristics:

(94) Props: Tables, menus, food, check, money

Roles: Customer, cook, owner, waiter, cashier

Entry Conditions: Customer is hungry.
Customer has money.

Results: Customer has less money.
          Customer is not hungry.
          Owner has more money.

Scenes:

1. Entering

    Customer goes into restaurant.

    Customer looks around.

    Customer decides where to sit.

    Customer goes to the table and sits down.

2. Ordering

    Customer picks up menus.

    Customer decides on food.

    Customer orders food from waiter.

    Waiter tells cook the order.

    Cook prepares food.

3. Eating

    Cook gives food to waiter.

    Waiter gives food to customer.

    Customer eats food.

4. Exiting

    Waiter writes out check.

    Waiter brings check to customer.

    Customer gives tip to waiter.

    Customer goes to cash register.

    Customer gives money to cashier.

Customer leaves restaurant.
(Schank and Abelson 1977)

Our frame for the event of *going to a restaurant* allows us to fill in the missing information:

(95) John walked into a restaurant. The waiter showed him to a table. He ordered a rare steak and a bottle of beer. As he left, he smiled at the waiter and the cashier.

It does not say explicitly whether John sat down, ate the steak and drank the beer he ordered, left a tip, paid his bill, and so on. But information about what must have happened can be retrieved by frame-based inferences. In (95), "John walked into a restaurant" provides a frame for the story told there.

Different frames generate different stories. Consider the way the story in the following example is framed by the topic sentence:

(96) "John is pretty crazy, and sometimes does strange things. Yesterday he went to Sardi's for dinner. He sat down, examined the menu, ordered a steak, and got up and left." (Brown and Yule 1983)

We tend to think and reason in terms of frames, but the stories we construct based on the existing frames do not necessarily represent the truth. Chua explains:

(97) FACTS VERSUS FRAME

A central tenet of frame theory is that when facts do not fit a person's frame, the fact is not internalized. As Lakoff writes, "If the truth doesn't fit the existing frame, the frame will stay in place and the truth will dissipate." If a person believes that taxes are an affliction, he or she might be less inclined to believe a report about how tax cuts can actually hurt the economy. Conversely, someone who believes that taxes are an investment in America is more likely to believe the report. In both cases, there is often a lack of critical questioning: if the fact doesn't fit the frame, it's ignored, and if the fact does fit the frame, it's accepted. This is not an indictment of human thought so much as it is a fact of how humans think.

There is a common myth that people, once faced with the bare facts, will be persuaded to side with the truth. In reality, the truth does not always set one free; rather, the truth matters most when it fits pre-existing worldviews and frames. This suggests that a persuasive tactic would be to change people's frames rather than present facts that conflict with their frames. (Chua 2006)

Lakoff's theory of framing can be applied not only to political issues (like taxation) but also to a person. For example, once a person has been framed in a certain way, it becomes very difficult for him or her to get out of the frame, as proved by the Rosenhan experiment. In this experiment, "eight sane people gained secret admission to twelve different hospitals," and although the "pseudopatients" tried to behave in a completely normal manner from the time of admission, the professional staff of the hospitals could not detect their sanity. Rosenhan writes, "Once a person is designated abnormal, all of his other behaviors and characteristics are colored by that label. Indeed, that label is so powerful that many of the pseudopatients' normal behaviors were overlooked entirely or profoundly misinterpreted." Moreover, "Having once been labeled schizophrenic, there is nothing the pseudopatient can do to overcome the tag. The tag profoundly colors others' perceptions of him and his behavior" (Rosenhan 1973). To frame a person is to perceive the person through the confines of a mental window. It is to embed the person in a story that fits our existing beliefs. And, since we are the author and narrator of the story, it is real to us, even if it is not true.

Narrative Connection

Before closing this chapter, let's revisit Velleman (2002):

> (98) There is no doubt but that stories, so defined, usually recount sequences of causally related events, and that the causal relations among narrated events lend both coherence and explanatory force to the story. But I am skeptical of Carroll's claim that all narrative connections, and all narrative explanations, are fundamentally causal. I think that connections of other kinds lend coherence and explanatory force to a story; and that it is these other connections that are constitutive of the narrative form. What I doubt, then, is whether causal connections account for the explanatory force that is essential to narrative. My skepticism is aroused, to begin with, by Carroll's example of a non-story. I agree with Carroll that he doesn't really tell a story when he says, "Aristarchus hypothesized the heliocentric theory thereby anticipating Copernicus' discovery by many centuries." Yet this sentence may fall short of being a story, not because it describes events that are causally

unrelated, but because it merely alludes to the second event by way of characterizing the first, without ever asserting that the second occurred. Even the shortest story must recount more than one event.

This account of Carroll's failure to tell a story does not apply to his second attempt, which goes like this: "Aristarchus hypothesized the heliocentric system and then centuries later Copernicus discovered it again." Here Carroll recounts two events, one after the other, and yet he claims that he still hasn't told a story. I don't know whether to accept this claim, but it is in any case considerably weaker than what Carroll is committed to claiming. For he is committed to claiming, not just that he hasn't told a story about Aristarchus and Copernicus, but that there is no true story to be told about them, given their mutual isolation in the web of causality. I am not convinced: I am fairly certain that one could tell a story about these events, and without inventing a causal connection between them. (Velleman 2002)

Stories involve a sequence of events rather than just a single event, and one definition of "story" is that it is an account of a set of events that are *causally* related. But (98) is casting doubt on the idea that causal connection is the *fundamental and indispensable* property of a story. If so, what determines the "storyness" of a story? Velleman (2002) seems to argue that, first of all, what is essential is the "explanatory force." In other words, whether something is a story depends on whether it has an explanatory force that makes meaningful the sequence of events described in it. What, then, lends explanatory force to a story, if it is not a causal connection? Here is Velleman's answer:

(99) Consider Aristotle's example of a causally disjointed story:

> Tragedy, however, is an imitation not only
> of a complete action, but also of incidents
> arousing pity and fear. Such incidents have
> the very greatest effect on the mind when they
> occur unexpectedly and at the same time in
> consequence of one another; there is more
> [of] the marvelous in them then than if they
> happened of themselves or by mere chance. Even
> matters of chance seem most marvelous if there
> is an appearance of design as it were in them; as
> for instance the statue of Mitys at Argos killed
> the author of Mitys' death by falling down on
> him when he was attending a public spectacle; for
> incidents like that we think to be not without a
> meaning. [*Poetics* §9, p. 1465]

> Here Aristotle is trying to reconcile the requirement
> that plotted events follow "by necessity or probability,"
> on the one hand, with the requirement that they
> arouse fear and pity, on the other, given that these
> emotions are enhanced by the element of surprise.
> The usual way to reconcile these requirements,
> according to Aristotle, is to have the plotted
> events "occur unexpectedly and at the same time
> in consequence of one another." Another way of
> obtaining the same effect, however, is for causally
> unrelated events to have what Aristotle calls "an

appearance of design," as when a murderer is accidentally killed by a statue of his victim.

Surely, the death of Mitys' murderer makes for a good story. We might interpret Aristotle as claiming that the "appearance of design" in this story is actually an appearance of causality, because the audience is led to imagine an avenging spirit behind the falling statue. But I think that the story holds up even under an absurdist reading, which takes the murderer's death for an accident. On this reading, the murder of Mitys and the death of his murderer are no more connected than the discoveries of Aristarchus and Copernicus. Even so, the one pair of disjointed events seems like more of a story than the other. Something is present in Aristotle's pair of events that's missing from Carroll's, and it needn't be an imagined causal connection. What is it?

A salient difference between these examples, I think, is that in Aristotle's the sequence of events completes an emotional cadence in the audience. When a murder is followed by a fitting comeuppance, we feel indignation gratified. Although these events follow no causal sequence, they provide an emotional resolution, and so they have a meaning for the audience, despite lacking any causal connection. No similar emotional cadence is resolved by Copernicus' rediscovery of what Aristarchus had previously discovered—not, at least, in Carroll's telling. The possibility in principle of fashioning these discoveries into a story is due to the possibility of finding something that they might

mean to an audience in emotional terms. Similarly
in Forster's example, the king's death need not
have contributed to the queen's in order to provide
materials for a story. Let the queen laugh at the
king's death and later slip on a fatal banana peel: the
audience will experience the resolution characteristic
of a plot. (Velleman 2002)

It is beyond both my abilities and the scope of this work to
define what a narrative connection is or to give a set of necessary and sufficient conditions for it to emerge. But the example
of a murderer being accidentally killed by a statue of his victim, and the analyses of it by Aristotle and by Velleman, seem
to have some relevance to our discussion on the emergence of
meaning in general.

(100) a. "We seem as a species to be driven by a desire
to make meanings. We are, above all, Homo
significans. Faced even by 'meaningless' patterns
the mind restlessly strives to make them
meaningful" (Chandler 1997).

b. The mind has a natural tendency to relate and
unite things that are located together, in an effort
to make the string or sequence meaningful.

c. We tend to prefer ( ) to) (because the former
is closed and the latter is open. Also, we are
psychologically uncomfortable with something
that is "incomplete" and does not bring us a sense
of "closure."

d. Both language and a person constitute conditions
for meaning to arise, and meaning arises as a
result of the interplay of these conditions.

e. The emergence of meaning m is a phenomenon that occurs with, and out of, the organic union or integration of the relevant conditions that support its emergence.

f. When meaning arises, there seems to exist some kind of integrative power that holds the relevant conditions in a state of union and supports the emergence of the meaning out of the union.

g. A human individual is an entity living and developing in a complex web of biological, physical, psychological, social, cultural, or other kinds of influences, and he or she brings those influences to a linguistic stimulus. In other words, those influences constitute conditions that affect whether, and how, the meaning of the stimulus emerges.

h. In a sense, meaning may be likened to a spark that is produced when flint and steel are struck together. Both flint and steel are necessary to the production of a spark, but neither of them is, by itself, a spark. And yet, a spark comes forth at the scene where flint and steel meet. Like a spark, meaning emerges when certain conditions are present, integrated, and working together as one. There is no emergence of meaning without conditions, and yet meaning itself cannot be found in any of the individual conditions. On another front, there should be enough heat for a spark to be generated, and the heat is a form of energy caused by the friction that occurs when flint and steel are struck together. Similarly, since meaning is not detectable if the conditions are examined singly or independently of each other, we might say that it originates with some kind of energy that is created when the conditions interact.

I'll share a personal experience here. I remember reading somewhere the following facts:

(101) a. Stevie Wonder was born prematurely.

    b. He was placed in an incubator for oxygen treatment.

    c. He was given too much oxygen because, at that time, no one knew that oxygen in high doses damaged newborns' eyes.

    d. This caused the child to suffer permanent blindness.

There are narrative connections in (101), from the first event, (101a), through the fourth, (101d). We can summarize (101) as this: *Stevie Wonder became blind shortly after his birth.* Now consider (102):

(102) Stevie Wonder was born on May 13, 1950, and became blind shortly after his birth.

Can we find a narrative connection between Stevie Wonder's birth and his becoming blind? Again, instead of answering with a simple yes or no, I prefer to say that there is *potentially* a narrative connection. I first learned of the facts stated in (102) a long time ago, probably when in my late teens. Then, years later, I read a story about Stevie Wonder that went something like this:

(103) Stevie's mother used to cry about his being so
talented and blind, and Stevie said, "Mother, maybe
God made me this way so that God could show
His wonders." At another time he also said that his
blindness was a blessing, allowing him to concentrate
on his sense of hearing.

Before I read (103), (102) was just a chronicle. But after
reading (103), I think I had a new understanding of the connection between Stevie Wonder's birth and his blindness. In other
words, with my knowledge of (103) as a condition, a narrative
meaning of (102) emerged. But how did (103) help (102) actualize its potential as a story? Why did (103) lend "explanatory
force" to (102)?

I believe it was both because

(104) a. (102) was embedded in a larger story, or context,
where the two events that occurred to Stevie
Wonder had "an appearance of (God's) design,"
and because

(104) b. I experienced something "emotional" (which I
could not put into words).

For (102) to become a story/narrative, (104a) was necessary
but not sufficient; (104b) was necessary as well (at least for me),
because at that time I had no real religious belief. What, then, I
wondered (and still wonder), was this emotional experience? It
might be labeled as an "emotional resolution," but I am not sure.
If it was an emotional resolution, it was a resolution to what? (I
do not want my audience to take this the wrong way here. I am
not challenging Velleman's argument, because I agree with him.

I am talking about my personal experience.) Maybe I am making much ado about nothing.

All I can say is that probably "emotional resolution" requires some degree of *reality* if it is to be effective. "God gave Stevie life and blindness so that He could show His wonders, and so Stevie was born on May 13, 1950, and became blind shortly after his birth." It is my feeling that in order for this to be a story or narrative, it needs to contain a certain level of reality. Otherwise, it is mere fiction and Stevie Wonder is fictional, not a human being like me, and so it does not really have a "meaning" for me.

Consider Oberlander and Lascarides's discussion:

(105) It has been observed in the literature (Harkness 1985; Hamann 1989) that some discourses set up an expectation of a contingent link between two eventualities, and that there are differing ways of responding to utterances which frustrate that expectation.

In particular, Hamann has observed that temporal connectives, such as *before, after,* and *when,* appear to have this effect:

The [temporal clause] event not only informs of time location but has a narrative relevance in its own right ... only some of [the many possible co-locating events] make sense in context ... total unconnectedness ... leads to a purely temporal reading, or to some profound statement about the way of the world brought about by the interpreter's willingness to see a narrative connection. (Hamann 1989, 43)

On her account ... (4b), by yoking the events together with an *after*-clause, carries an additional implicature that the leaving was contingent upon the homecoming perhaps by being caused by it. The fact that *after* leads to such an expectation is involved in the explanation of the oddness of (5).

(4) [...]

b. Mary left after John came home.

(5) ? The moon eclipsed the sun after John came home.

The explanation goes along the following lines. Sentences of the form *A after B* usually link eventualities which can cause one another, where B is a clause, but not when it is an adverb. However, we also have a strong prior intuition that eclipses are not contingent on human activities. When a conflict like this arises, we either (i) derive a purely temporal reading; or (ii) derive a "profound" reading. Following strategy (i), we would read (5) as simply locating the solar eclipse at a time after the time of the homecoming; here, the clause *after John came home* is functioning just as *after 7pm* would function. Following strategy (ii), we would read (5) as pointing out a new and surprising fact about the world; there is a human whose movements influence planetary motion. (Oberlander and Lascarides 2000)

For "The moon eclipsed the sun after John came home" to be a story/narrative to me, I need to be a "profound" reader as well as be willing to see a narrative connection in Hamann-speak between the two events described in the example. But even if I am willing to see a narrative connection, the "profound" reading is unrealistic. It is unrealistic if "John" is a human being like me. And if I try to see a narrative connection, he needs to be a fictional person (for example, in a science fiction novel).

Now, I said earlier, "With my knowledge of (103) as condition, a narrative meaning of (102) emerged." I think there was something grounded and real in that narrative meaning that I could make a connection to, or there was a certain level of reality in it that people in general could relate to on an emotional level. We are always looking for meaning. And, whether consciously or unconsciously, we are looking for answers to such questions as "Why are we?" "What is fate?" "Who decides?" "Do we have to resign ourselves to our fate?" This desire for meaning makes Stevie's story our own. With our desire for meaning as condition, narrative connection and its reality emerge.

Deep down, I think that I, too, have been looking for answers to such questions as those above. I said earlier that after reading (103), I think I had a "new" understanding of the connection between Stevie Wonder's birth and his blindness. But understanding of narrative connection is always "new" with each new phase we enter. Each of us is an entity living and developing in a complex web of influences, and those influences constitute conditions that affect how narrative meaning emerges.

In my mid-twenties, I encountered the concepts of go (karma) and ganken ogo (literally, "to assume (bad) karma of one's own volition"). In layman's terms, ganken ogo means, "We choose our sufferings in order to show proof of a victorious life. We need not be victims. We are voluntarily undergoing hardships to show others the path to a victorious life." With this idea as condition, a new narrative connection and its powerful reality emerged. Then, in my late twenties, I was admitted to graduate school to study linguistics, which I have been studying for the past twenty years. Right now, as I work on this section, I find myself recalling a Buddhist parable of a man shot and wounded by a poisoned arrow. He insists on knowing who shot him, with what kind of arrow fletched with what kind of feather, the nature of the poison, and so on, before having the arrow pulled out and the wound cleaned. At the same time, I also find myself recalling the story of Helen Keller, who "was born on June 27, 1880, and lost her sight and hearing at the age of nineteen months." Here is a passage from her autobiography:

(106) We walked down the path to the well-house, attracted by the fragrance of the honeysuckle with which it was covered. Some one was drawing water and my teacher placed my hand under the spout. As the cool stream gushed over one hand she spelled into the other the word water, first slowly, then rapidly. I stood still, my whole attention fixed upon the motions of her fingers. Suddenly I felt a misty consciousness as of something forgotten—a thrill of returning thought; and somehow the mystery of language was revealed to me. I knew then that "w-a-t-e-r" meant the wonderful cool something that was flowing over my hand. That living word awakened my soul, gave it light, hope, joy, set it free! (Keller 1903)

Since doing linguistic research is part of my regular vocation, I am incessantly asking myself metalinguistic questions. But if I should allow myself to become fixated on questions of abstract theory and ideology to the exclusion of all else, the "poison of the arrow" would pass into my system before my questions are ever answered. The meaning of "water" suddenly emerged as Anne spelled the word into one hand of Helen *and* the real pump water gushed over her other hand. That was how the connection between language, meaning, and person was made. The same would apply to narrative connection. It is not something that can be found in the ink marks on a page, or electronic characters on a screen. It is not something that can be discussed divorced from the reality we experience from within. Helen Keller also said, "Alone we can do so little; together we can do so much." Meaning does not arise due to a single factor or condition. The emergence of the meaning of "water," I imagine, was like the spark that is produced when flint and steel are struck together. It originated with the energy that was created when the teacher and the student interacted.

The sentences "Stevie Wonder was born on May 13, 1950, and became blind shortly after his birth" and "Helen Keller was born on June 27, 1880, and lost her sight and hearing at the age of nineteen months" are linguistic stimuli and conditions. And they are potentially stories; there are potentially narrative connections between the two juxtaposed events in each sentence. The narrative potentials are actualized depending on various other relevant conditions, of which the reader is part, and their integration with the linguistic conditions. Everyone has some kind of problem to deal with—at least, I do (a lot). It is my conclusion, then, that the narrative connections and stories will manifest themselves in the process of my actual struggle to overcome my problems, one after another. The narrative meanings will emerge in the process of making my own *ganken ogo* stories happen.

4

Rethinking
"Two Female Students—A Headache for Professor Yamamoto"
from the Perspective of Speech Act Theory

Based on the discussion thus far, this chapter presents a pragmatic analysis of "Two Female Students—A Headache for Professor Yamamoto," a slightly modified version of an actual *shukanshi* magazine headline, from the perspective of speech act theory. After first describing the theory, we will then apply it to the analysis of the (modified) headline.

Pragmatics and Speech Act Theory

First of all, what does it mean to analyze language pragmatically? In order to answer this question, let's look at a concrete example. What does the following utterance mean?

(107) "Do you know what time it is?"

If a nonnative speaker of English says that it means *Ima nanji ka wakaru?* (Japanese) or *Sa che ore sono?* (Italian), this suggests that the person has enough knowledge of English syntax and semantics to analyze this sentence. But a pragmatist would not be satisfied with this answer. Pragmatists are interested in more than just the literal meaning of the sentence; they are more interested in what the speaker *intended to convey* by uttering (107). Pragmatists think, for example, that the interrogative sentence may have been used to make a request equivalent to "Tell me what time it is," or even that it may have been used as a reproach equivalent to "You are very late."

One of the contributions that pragmatists have made to the field of linguistics is the discrimination between two different levels of meaning:

(108) Two Levels of Meaning:

1. sentence meaning (literal, or semantic, meaning)

2. utterance meaning (speaker's, or conveyed, meaning)

Another important contribution made by pragmatists is that they draw people's attention to the crucial role that *contexts* play in interpreting an utterance. For example, as we just saw in the example of "Do you know what time it is?" the same sentence may be used for at least two different purposes in two different contexts. In other words, the way language is used has much to do with the context in which it is employed. Basically, pragmatics concerns context-dependent meaning of an utterance.

One of the most important theories that contributed to the rise of present-day pragmatics is speech act theory, which was developed by the English linguistic philosopher John L. Austin. The essential point made in the theory is that "language is action."

(109) Language is action.

When we speak, we act.

We act through language.

To say something is to do something (Austin 1962).

What does "Language is action" mean? We can approach this question by comparing the following two sentences:

(110) a. Since I was afraid, I hid myself.

b. Since you want to know, I saw Max with your wife.

What does the "since-clause" in each of the above sentences modify; that is, how does it relate to the main clause? In (110a), the since-clause is directly related to the content expressed in the main clause. That is to say, (110a) means that the speaker's fear caused him to hide himself. But in (110b), the same logico-semantic relationship of causality cannot be expressed, because at the time of the sentence's utterance, the hearer's desire to know is not the cause of the speaker's having seen Max with the hearer's wife. In other words, the fact conveyed in the main clause is *independent*, in terms of causality, of the fact conveyed in the since-clause. The same observation can be made about (111):

(111) There are biscuits on the sideboard if you want them.

In this case, too, we can observe that the actual presence of the biscuits is not conditional on, or related to, the hearer's desire to eat them (Sweetser 1990).

How, then, do the since-clause in (110b) and the if-clause in (111) relate to their main clauses respectively? To answer this question, let us first consider cases where a subordinate clause is accompanied not by a "linguistic" main clause but by nonverbal communication. Suppose a person named Mary is asked by her old friend John to lend him a hundred dollars, and she gives him the money, saying,

(112) a. "If you are so badly in need of money…"

    b. "Since you are an old friend of mine…"

    c. "Although I don't have much money to spare…"

Or suppose that at a later date, John happens to see Mary and gives the money back to her, saying,

(112) d. "Oh, before I forget…"

In these cases, can we say that the utterances are complete? The utterances introduced here are subordinate clauses and lack main clauses, so, syntactically speaking, they are incomplete. But in the case of (112d), for example, after Mary receives the money, it would not be appropriate for her to say, "By the way, what were you about to say when you mentioned, 'Before I forget'?" And the same is true for the other utterances in (112). For example, in the case of (112a), after receiving the money, it would be inappropriate for John to say, "By the way, what were you about to say when you mentioned, 'If you are so badly in need of money'?" That being the case, we should conclude that the utterances in (112) are complete as they are.

Then what makes them complete? In the case of utterances (a) to (c), it is the act of the speaker giving the money, and in the case of (d), it is the act of the speaker returning the money. In other words, the act of giving the money or returning the money plays the role of the main clause.

Now, let's temporarily call this phenomenon "the integration of language with action," since the subordinate clauses are combined with the act of giving or returning the money and thereby become "complete" in terms of communication.

Note in passing that when the integration of language and action occurs, language need not necessarily *precede* action. There may be cases where the two overlap. Or, as (113) illustrates, it is possible that action may precede language, just as it is also possible that action may be sandwiched between two different utterances that take the form of subordinate clauses.

(113) a. [Mary gives the money to John] *Mary:* Since you are an old friend of mine...

<Action—Language>

b. *Mary:* Although I don't have much money to spare... [Mary gives the money to John] *Mary:* Since you are an old friend of mine...

<Language—Action—Language>

So far, we have talked about how language and action are combined and work together. I used the term "integration," meaning "the integration of language and action." Now, this terminology might give the false impression that I view language and action as two distinct, or separate, entities, because "to integrate" can be defined as "to bring together separate parts or things into a unified and harmonious whole." But using language—or, to put it plainly, saying something—is also an action.

In what sense, then, is saying something, in itself, an action? We can respond to this question with two answers:

(114) *Jack:* [to his mother] I am hungry. (Mori 1987)

If I ask,

(115) what is Jack, the speaker in (114), *doing?*

what is the answer? Note that my concern is not what Jack is *saying* but what he is *doing.*

In response to the question, we can say, at one level, that Jack is performing the act of producing a series of sounds consisting of "ai æm hʌŋgri (I am hungry)," and at another level, we can say that he is performing the act of requesting that his mother prepare him a meal.

(116) a. the act of producing a series of sounds consisting
of "ai æm hʌŋgri (I am hungry)"

b. the act of requesting that his mother prepare him a
meal

Now, in speech act theory, the two acts described in (116a) and (116b) are termed a "locutionary act" and an "illocutionary act" respectively. A locutionary act is, simply, the act of saying or uttering something. Actually, a locutionary act can be divided into three subtypes: phonetic, phatic, and rhetic acts. But for our purposes here, it will suffice to say,

(117) a locutionary act is the act of uttering a series of
sounds that have meaning.

(118) An illocutionary act, on the other hand, is the act
that a speaker performs in uttering words.

So when we say something, we are not just performing a locutionary act; that is, we are not just performing the act of producing sounds by using our vocal cords. We are also performing
another, illocutionary, act. And in the case of example (114), the
illocutionary act performed by Jack is the act of requesting a
meal. In other words, when Jack says, "I am hungry," he is performing locutionary and illocutionary acts simultaneously.

By the way, "illocutionary" is a term coined by Austin, who
added the prefix "il-" to "locutionary" to form the new word.
The original form of the prefix is "in-," but it is changed to "il-"
instead of preserving the original form. In this orthographical
transformation, the process known as *assimilation* is involved.
The "n" of the prefix "in" has been assimilated with the first letter
in "locutionary," which is "l." Notice here that since a locutionary act is the act of saying, or uttering, something, an illocutionary act can be described as what the speaker is doing *in* saying
or uttering something.

Therefore, if we try to formulate the relationship between
the two acts, the formula would be something like this: "In saying X, the speaker is doing Y [or Y-ing]" (Austin 1962).

(119) In saying X, the speaker is doing Y [or Y-ing].

saying X = locutionary act

doing Y [or Y-ing] = illocutionary act

And if we apply this formula to example (114), we can get
(120a').

(120) a. *Jack:* [to his mother] I am hungry. (= 114)

    a'. In saying, "I am hungry," Jack is requesting that his mother prepare him a meal.

Now it's time to return to the question posed earlier in (110):

(121) What does the since-clause in the following sentence modify, or how does it relate to its main clause?
Since you want to know, I saw Max with your wife.

Let's first apply the formula that we just introduced to the main clause of this sentence:

(122) In saying, "I saw Max with your wife," the speaker is informing the hearer that he or she saw Max with the hearer's wife.

Based on (122), we can see that in uttering the main clause, the speaker is performing an act of *informing* the hearer that he or she saw Max with the hearer's wife, and it is this illocutionary act that the since-clause in (121) is related to. In other words, the since-clause gives the reason why the speaker *tells* the hearer that the speaker saw Max with the hearer's wife, and not the reason why the speaker *saw* Max with the hearer's wife.

We can use two more examples to better illustrate the notion of illocutionary acts:

(123) *Tom:* The earth is flat.

    Harry: That's false.

What does the demonstrative pronoun "that" in Harry's utterance refer to? In this case, "that" refers to the propositional content of the sentence Tom has just uttered.

(124) *Tom:* You're an idiot.

Harry: *That*'s not very kind of you.

In this case, "that" refers to the act that Tom has just performed, that is, the act of insulting Harry. In other words, in saying, "You're an idiot," Tom has performed the illocutionary act of insulting Harry, and "that" in Harry's utterance refers to this unkind act of insult done by Tom.

Let's look at the following conversation from the perspective of speech act theory:

(125) *Tom:* [to Harry] What are you, stupid or something?

Dick: Yeah, yeah!

Harry: That's not very kind of you!

We can make four observations about this conversation: (1) Although Tom's utterance takes the form of a question, Tom is not really requiring an answer from Harry. Rather, in saying, "What are you, stupid or something?" he is, again, insulting Harry. (2) Following Tom's utterance, Dick chimes in, saying, "Yeah, yeah!" To put it another way, in saying, "Yeah, yeah!" Dick has joined Tom in performing an illocutionary act of insulting Harry. (3) In saying, "That's not very kind of you!" Harry is reproaching both Tom and Dick for their insulting illocutionary acts. (4) The demonstrative pronoun "that" in Harry's utterance refers to Tom's and Dick's illocutionary acts of insult.

Finally, look at (126):

(126) A: Where should we eat out?

B: Well, Edoya has great sushi, *but* Meijiya has excellent tempura.

In this example, why is "but" used to join "Edoya has great sushi" and "Meijiya has excellent tempura"? Do the two conjuncts clash in any way? (Is there any contradiction between the two facts that Edoya has great sushi and that Meijiya has excellent tempura?) In answering the question, let's first consider (127a):

(127) a. *A:* Where should we eat out?

B: Edoya has great sushi.

In this context, in saying, "Edoya has great sushi," speaker B is making the suggestion "We should go to Edoya restaurant." Similarly, in (127b) below, speaker B is making the suggestion "We should go to Meijiya restaurant."

(127) b. *A:* Where should we eat out?

B: Meijiya has excellent tempura.

But the suggestion of going to eat at Edoya and the suggestion of going to eat at Meijiya cannot be followed simultaneously, and therefore, the two suggestions clash if they are made at the same time. Speaker B in (126) is aware of this. Speaker B is aware that "Edoya has great sushi" and "Meijiya has excellent tempura" contradict each other in terms of "illocutionary act," and so speaker B has used the conjunction "but" to join the two conjuncts. By the way, one could argue that regardless of which conjunction you use to join them, the act of proposing two mutually exclusive options simultaneously is, in itself, inappropriate. But that isn't the case at all—it is just one way of offering more than one possibility and allowing the hearer to choose between them (Sweetser 1990).

Now, I would like to look further into an intricate aspect of the illocutionary act. To begin with, let's revisit this example:

(128) *Jack:* [to his mother] I am hungry. (= 114)

According to the discussion so far, in this example, Jack is performing the illocutionary act of *requesting* that his mother prepare him a meal, and there is nothing wrong with this analysis. But on second thought, isn't it possible, in the first place, to say that Jack is performing an illocutionary act of *informing* his mother that he is hungry, or an illocutionary act of *asserting* that he is hungry? Of course that is possible, because *informing* and *asserting* are both considered to be illocutionary acts.

(129) a. Jack is performing an illocutionary act of
    informing or *asserting* that he is hungry.

   b. Jack is performing an illocutionary act of
    requesting that his mother prepare him a meal.

What conclusions can we draw from this observation? First of all, we can say that more than one illocutionary act could be performed at the same time through the same single utterance.

(130) The same utterance could perform multiple
    illocutionary acts at once.

This then leads us to wonder what the various relationships are between the multiple illocutionary acts. To find an answer to this question, we should look at it from the aspect of how direct the connection is between the utterance and each of the illocutionary acts being performed.

In the example "I am hungry," there seems to be a straightforward relationship between the words uttered and the act of informing the speaker's mother that he is hungry. On the other hand, what about the connection between the utterance and the act of requesting that his mother prepare a meal? The connection here seems less direct. First, there is no linguistic connection here, because the utterance itself makes no mention of a meal or of preparing it. Second, as is shown in (131), the illocutionary act of requesting a meal is performed *by way of* the illocutionary act of informing the speaker's mother of his hunger.

(131) In saying, "I am hungry," Jack is requesting a meal *by way of* informing the hearer that he is hungry.

In other words, in this example, Jack is *indirectly* requesting a meal.

Actually, we can find examples like this quite often in everyday conversations—examples of *indirect illocutionary acts*, or cases where the speaker is performing one illocutionary act by way of performing another.

(132) [On a crowded train] *Passenger A:* [to passenger B] You are standing on my foot.

Here passenger A is performing an indirect illocutionary act of requesting passenger B to get off his or her foot, by way of asserting that passenger B is standing on his or her foot.

(133) *Tim:* Let's go to the movies tonight.

Sue: I have to study for an exam.

Here Sue is indirectly refusing Tim's invitation to the movies by way of making the statement that she has to study for an exam.

Note that an indirect illocutionary act is not necessarily realized through uttering a declarative sentence such as "You are standing on my foot" or "I have to study for an exam."

(134) [A husband and wife are sitting at the dining room
table, eating a meal.]
Husband: Can you reach the salt?

Here the husband is asking a question using an interrogative form, and in speech act theory, asking a question is also an
example of an illocutionary act, along with asserting, ordering,
promising, and so on. Thus, (134) can be analyzed as follows: In
saying, "Can you reach the salt?" the husband is asking a question about his wife's ability to reach the salt. But in this context,
it is clear that he is also performing the illocutionary act of requesting that his wife pass him the salt. In other words, (134) is
an example of the speaker indirectly requiring the hearer to do
something, by means of asking a question (Searle 1979).

Finally, let us consider this example again:

(135) There are biscuits on the sideboard if you want them.
(= 111)

In this case, in uttering the main clause, the speaker is performing an illocutionary act of offering biscuits by way of informing the hearer that there are biscuits on the sideboard, and
it is this indirect illocutionary act of offering that relates to the
if-clause in (135). Illocutions are like the air we breathe: they are
there, but usually we are not aware of their being performed at
the conscious level.

Now, although speech act theory is traditionally associated
with oral speech, the notion "language is action" can be applied
to written texts as well. And in that case, the following corre-
spondence relation could be established:

(136) a. The locutionary act would correspond to the act of producing and communicating written text (on paper, computer screen, and so on).

b. The illocutionary act would correspond to the act performed in the production and communication of the written text.

How, then, does the speech act theory work when applied to the *shukanshi* magazine headline in (137), which is the focus in this study?

(137) a. Two Female Students—A Headache for Professor Yamamoto [Headline]

b. Rumor is that two female students in Professor Yamamoto's seminar class are on bad terms. This must be causing a headache for him. [Article Summary]

(137a) is a slightly modified version of an actual headline, but it is substantially the same as the original in that it is misleading in the same way. Also, it is worthy of analysis because it is a typical example of the type of misleading headline frequently used in certain national *shukanshi* magazines. Let's take a hard look at what the editor or headline writer has done, whether directly or indirectly, in delivering (137a) to the public.

Two Female Students—A Headache for Professor Yamamoto

To begin with, let's restate below the analysis that we made of (137a) in the first section of chapter 3:

(138) First, we are influenced by the very fact that it is a *shukanshi* magazine headline. This is because, when a dog bites a man, that is not news, since it happens so often. But if a man bites a dog, that is news. We expect the article to be about something scandalous or shocking. This expectation then gives rise to certain assumptions. For example, is Professor Yamamoto male or female? We can't tell. Yet the headline leads us to infer strongly, or almost presuppose, that the professor is male. Next, in what way are the students a headache for the professor? Although each word in (137a) by itself does not say for certain, the headline as a whole creates a false image of the professor as being involved in a romantic relationship with both students.

The article under the headline is simply about a human relations problem, but our interpretation of the headline is influenced by how each party is introduced—and the magazine's editor is well aware of it. For example, why has the editor chosen "two *female* students" instead of "two students"? Because he knows that just by his choices and arrangements of words, he can manipulate the reader's associations and let the activated associations interact. He knows that the reader constructs a story on the basis of the linguistic stimuli presented in the headline—a story in which the "womanizing" professor is found out by his two student "lovers" and faces their angry reproaches—and he anticipates that the reader will be tempted to buy the magazine for the full story.

Simply stated, in producing and publishing the headline, the editor has

(139) successfully prompted the reader to construct
the story mentioned at the end of (138). (I say
"successfully" because, in personal interview surveys
and in my lecture to a group of men and women in
my community, I asked more than a hundred people
how they would interpret the headline, and almost
everyone interpreted it in more or less the same way
that I did in [138].)

But the matter is not quite so simple. Let's further analyze
what the editor has done:

(140) a. The editor knew that his or her choices and
arrangements of words would lead the reader to
construct the story.

b. The editor also knew that the story the reader
would construct was untrue.

In other words, the editor has lied. Or, more precisely,

(141) The editor has lied by way of guiding the reader to
construct a story that is untrue.

Merriam-Webster's 11th Collegiate Dictionary (2003) defines
the act of lying as follows:

(142) **lie** 1 a : an assertion of something known or believed
by the speaker to be untrue with intent to deceive

The "assertion" the editor has made is the headline Two Female Students—A Headache for Professor Yamamoto, but it has
given rise to the story that contains false assertions such as "The
professor is involved in a romantic relationship with both students," and "The professor was found out by the students and
now faces their reproaches." Therefore, we can replace the word

"assertion" in (142) with "story" and argue that the editor has lied by indirectly communicating the false story to the reader.

The editor might argue that he did not mislead the reader *intentionally*, and so he did not really "lie." He might argue against (140a) saying that he was not aware of it. But if his claim were true, he would not have become an editor in the first place, because his claim means he has no sense of how his words affect his readers. Also, although we cannot get inside a person's head, language can provide a "window into the human mind." For example, in discussing linguistic signals that indicate possible deception found in the statements from criminal suspects, Clark (1999) writes,

> (143) Another example of an unnecessary connection can be found in the following statement. "...*we got back in the car and got off exit 9 up to route 25 and called his girlfriend then called the police afterwards.*"
>
> This connection, *afterwards,* clearly shows that significant information is missing from the statement at that point. This term is unnecessary and even adds wordiness to the statement. It would have been sufficient for the subject to say "...we got back in the car and got off exit 9 up to route 25 and called his girlfriend and the police." The use of the unnecessary connection "afterwards" indicated that the subject intentionally left something out of the statement at that point....
>
> Other linguistic signals, which indicate missing information, are verbs that show that there was a certain break in activity. Words used by a subject such as *started, began, commenced, continued, proceeded, resumed, completed, finished,* and *ended* are clear indications that there was a break in a particular activity. This may indicate

that information is missing at that particular place in the statement. However, if the subject indicates within the statement why there was a certain break in the activity, then you can disregard the connection.

The following statements show the difference between a statement which indicates a break in activity that is explained within the narrative, and one which indicates a break in activity that is not explained or understood by the reader.

"I got home from work at 5:00 and started to make dinner. I was interrupted with a telephone call from my mother who invited me to her house for dinner that evening. I dropped everything and went over to her house at about 5:30." With this statement, the reader understands that she started dinner, but did not complete it, and it is explained why within the statement.

However, in the following statement we see a different situation. *"She asked me if I wanted to go with her and I said 'no.' So she left then I sat down and <u>started</u> watching TV. I don't remember what show I was watching."* In this particular statement, the subject *started* watching, which clearly shows that this was interrupted by something, but it is not explained within the statement. This is an indication that the subject intentionally omitted information at this point. Furthermore, the term used by this subject *"I don't remember"* in an open statement is another indication that information is intentionally being suppressed and increases the probability that deception is present. Combining both the verb *started* and the phrase *"I don't remember,"* we begin to see a cluster of deceptive indicators present within this narrative. (Clark 1999)

Similarly, the editor's language is a guide to his intention. For example, like the term "afterwards" in Clark's example, the word "female" in the headline is unnecessary. It would have been sufficient for him to write, Two Students—a Headache for Professor Yamamoto. This added information on the two students' sex clearly shows his intention to mislead the reader. He wanted the reader to construct a particular story based on his headline, and this story was different from the one that would be constructed based on the headline without the sex information.

Second, we should pay keen attention to what the editor has done at a deeper level. In the previous chapter, we discussed humans' tendency to use stories to understand and interpret our world, and saw that the following human traits lie behind this tendency:

(144) a. We are *Homo narrans,* or storytelling creatures.

b. We are *Homo significans,* or meaning-makers.

c. We have an affinity for semantic gestalt.

d. We are an inference-making species.

e. We tend to think and reason in terms of frames.

(145) Therefore, in making the reader construct the false story, the magazine editor has manipulated and exploited basic human nature for a self-serving purpose (e.g., to increase sales).

Third, we should be aware of how the headline's suggestive wording can affect our memory. Suppose person A saw the headline in the magazine's advertisement on the train on his way to work, went for a drink with his colleague B after work, and started gossiping about the professor:

(146) "You know what? Some professor named Yamamoto slept with two of his students."

Empirically, this is something that is likely to happen. The question is,

(147) At the time of his uttering (146), was A simply inferring that the professor slept with the students? Or did he mistakenly assume that the information was actually in the headline he saw that morning?

To deal with this question, consider (148):

(148) ... Loftus and Palmer (1974) showed participants a movie depicting a traffic accident. Later, participants were asked to estimate how fast the cars were traveling at the time of the accident. Some participants were asked, "How fast were the cars going when they *smashed into* each other?" while others were asked "How fast were the cars going when they *hit* each other?" and still others were asked the same question with the verb *collided, bumped* or *contacted.* The particular verb made a difference in participants' speed estimates. For example, participants estimated that the car traveled faster in response to the word *smashed* than the word *hit.* In a second experiment using a similar method, participants were also asked if they had seen any broken glass at the accident scene. Those participants who had estimated the car's speed after hearing the word *smashed* were more likely to say that they had seen broken glass than those who had heard the word *hit*—yet there was no broken glass in the event. This research shows that leading questions can

affect people's reports immediately, and change their memories for event details later. Leading questions can act as PEI (Author's note: postevent information), telegraphing new details to participants either directly or indirectly. Later, when participants recall the event, their memories can be distorted by the information in the questions. (Gerrie, Garry, and Loftus 2005)

To describe the second experiment in more detail: (1) The participants were 150 students of the University of Washington. (2) They were shown a one-minute film that contained a four-second scene of a multiple-car crash. (3) They were divided into three groups, each with fifty participants. (4) The first group was asked, "How fast were the cars going when they *smashed* into each other?" The second group was asked, "How fast were the cars going when they *hit* each other?" The third group (control group) was not asked about the speed of the cars. (5) One week later, they were brought back to the laboratory to answer a series of questions (this time without viewing the film). The critical question was, "Did you see any broken glass?" and it was placed in a random position on each participant's question paper. (6) Although there was actually no broken glass in the film, the number of participants who erroneously "remembered" seeing broken glass was sixteen in the first group, seven in the second group, and six in the third group.

As we saw in chapter 3, we tend to think and reason in terms of frames. We have a frame for an event (as well as for an object, person, action, and so on), and we tend to "fill in" information about what may have happened, by making frame-based inferences. For example, the *accident occurring at a low speed* frame would evoke a story in which bumpers are scratched or fenders are dented. By the same token, reacting to the linguistic stimuli "when the cars *smashed* into each other" would not only result in a higher speed estimate but would also insinuate "details" such as broken glass, injuries of some degree, and so on, using a frame-based knowledge structure.

The suggestive wording of the headline in question has the effect of framing the professor as a "womanizer" and of inviting the reader to infer or create "narrative details" within that frame. In other words, the reader is led to fill in missing details based on the frame-based inferences about what the professor must have done. Therefore,

> (149) In leading readers to construct the false story, it is possible that the editor has led them to "mentally witness" nonexistent details.

The most important point in Loftus and Palmer's second experiment, however, is that the *smashed* question affected the *memories* of one-third of the participants in the first group. The verb "smashed," through the activation of the *accident occurring at a high speed* frame, insinuated broken glass into their memories.

Similarly, the headline's suggestive wording (especially the addition of the word "female" before "students") can affect the reader's memory. It is possible that the reader has inferred "nonexistent details" and that the inferred details, in turn, have crept into and become part of their memories. Therefore,

> (150) In using suggestive wording in the headline, it is possible that the editor has implanted false memories in the reader's mind.

Fourth, recall what we discussed earlier about conditioned emergence of meaning. (See also chapter 2 in this book.)

(151) a. A linguistic unit such as a word, phrase, clause, sentence, or text has—in short, language has—meaning potentials. But language cannot actualize its meaning potentials on its own or by itself; rather, it functions as a stimulus for its meaning to transform from potential to actual. In that sense, language serves as a "condition" for its own meaning potentials to emerge into a manifest state. Another important condition for the actualization of meaning potentials is the "recipient" of the linguistic stimuli.

    b. A human being serves as a condition for the actualization of the meaning potentials of language by receiving and responding to linguistic stimuli. But at the actual scene of the emergence of meaning, a variety of other conditions are found to be at work and to affect the way language is processed. These conditions are the conditions that coexist with human beings or pertain to human nature, and they may support or hinder the emergence of meaning.

In this connection, consider (152):

(152) When participants find the source of the PEI less credible, they tend to pay more attention and are misled less often. Dodd and Bradshaw (1980) showed participants a slide sequence of two cars involved in an accident, and then asked them to read a summary of the accident. They were told either

that the summary was prepared by a neutral witness, or by the driver that caused the accident. Of course, the narrative was prepared by the experimenter and was always the same misleading account of the accident. Participants were more likely to be misled by the neutral account than by the (seemingly biased) driver's account. These results suggest that when the "misinformation messenger" is a person of questionable reliability, participants show increased discrepancy detection. (Gerrie, Garry, and Loftus 2005)

Many of the Japanese *shukanshi* magazines that intentionally and repeatedly run misleading headlines like the one we are discussing can be categorized as "tabloid" magazines. But many people, including many who are considered to be intellectuals, are influenced by them. (Furthermore, there even have been cases where some politicians used information from these magazines to attack their political opponents.) This means,

(153) People know that some *shukanshi* magazines are not credible, and yet they are influenced by the magazines.

Why is this? Why are people so easily influenced by the headlines of those magazines, whose credibility is poor? To help pave the way to answering this question, let us first consider the following examples from Anderson et al. (1977):

(154) a. Every Saturday night four good friends get together. When Jerry, Mike, and Pat arrived, Karen was sitting in her living room writing some notes. She quickly gathered the cards and stood up to

greet her friends at the door. They followed her into the living room but as usual they couldn't agree on exactly what to play. Jerry eventually took a stand and set things up. Finally, they began to play. Karen's recorder filled the room with soft and pleasant music. Early in the evening, Mike noticed Pat's hand and the many diamonds. As the night progressed the tempo of play increased. Finally, a lull in the activities occurred. Taking advantage of this, Jerry pondered the arrangement in front of him. Mike interrupted Jerry's reverie and said, "Let's hear the score." They listened carefully and commented on their performance. When the comments were all heard, exhausted but happy, Karen's friends went home.

b. Rocky slowly got up from the mat, planning his escape. Things were not going well. What bothered him most was being held, especially since the charge against him had been weak. He considered his present situation. The lock that held him was strong, but he thought he could break it. Rocky was aware that it was because of his early roughness that he had been penalized so severely. The situation was becoming frustrating; the pressure had been grinding on him for too long. He was being ridden unmercifully. Rocky was getting angry now. He felt ready to make his move. He knew his success or failure would depend on what he did in the next few seconds. (Anderson et al. 1977)

Two groups of college sophomores read these passages. One of the groups consisted of female music majors, and the other of male physical education majors. It is reported that 71 percent of the music majors interpreted (154a) as being about a musical evening among friends, while the same percentage of the physical education majors interpreted it as being about four friends getting together for an evening of playing cards. Also, after reading (154b), 72 percent of the former group thought it was about a prison break, while 64 percent of the latter group thought it was about a wrestling match (Reynolds 2002). These experiments and their results show that (1) each passage in (154) has two meaning potentials; and (2) the actualization of the meaning potentials seems to be influenced by the readers' interests and prior experience. To put it in more general terms, such factors as readers' interests and prior experience can support the emergence of one meaning and help *prevent* the emergence of other possible meanings.

Similarly, how we interpret the headline in question partly depends on what we bring to it. We are interested in scandals. Scandals capture our attention and entertain us. We know that magazines are basically about entertainment and that we cannot take everything written in them as truth. We know that much of what is said in certain *shukanshi* magazines is meant to whet our appetite for scandal. And yet, we are sometimes tempted to hear what satisfies our appetite regardless of the credibility of the source, and to believe the scandal—in the case of the headline we are discussing, the "scandal" implied by the headline's wording—on the basis that "where there's smoke, there's fire."

It could be said, then, that the reader's appetite for scandal is one factor or condition that supports the emergence of the "scandalous story." In other words, the story was generated by the interaction between the external stimulus (the headline) and one of our inner negative tendencies. And since the editor is the provider of the misleading and suggestive headline, he or she has

> (155) successfully prompted the reader to construct the false and scandalous story, by stimulating a negative aspect of human nature.

I should add, however, that all the human qualities that are generally considered negative, including a taste for, or curiosity about, scandal, are inherent in us and cannot be eradicated. Depending on the individual, some qualities may be more pronounced or dominant than others, but every negative quality exists in all of us, at least potentially. Also, looked at from a different angle, what are considered negative qualities are inherent in our nature because they are necessary for us.

For example, there is a propensity in our nature to desire things that bring us pleasure, satisfaction, enjoyment, profit, and so on. Often this propensity is understood in terms of craving, greed, avarice, or covetousness, and so it is associated with negativity. But in and of itself, the propensity is not a bad thing. We have desires for food and sleep, for example, and while eating and sleeping are enjoyable activities, they are also necessary for survival. We may desire sex because it brings pleasure, but the desire is also necessary for the continuation of our genes, of mankind.

We have an element of animality, which is characterized by fear of the strong and oppression of the weak. This element is easy to view negatively, but it, too, is necessary, because it is associated with the instinct to flee from danger and protect and preserve our own lives and the lives of those close to us. Moreover, the "negative" characteristics can function in positive ways, too. Greed provides a powerful motivation and engine that make us take action to obtain what we need or want. If we use our desires arising from greed without harming others or resorting to unethical means, they can be the driving force to achieving good and meaningful things in life. Indeed, if properly managed, such desires can also work to the benefit of society as a whole. Anger, too, is considered a negative force or energy, because the emotion is associated with the instinct to fight or attack. But if it is directed (and expressed appropriately) toward injustice or evil, anger can manifest its positive aspect.

The problem with the headline is that it has stimulated and affected our nature as humans in a negative way. And the problem with the editor is that he or she has manipulated and exploited our nature to serve the editor's commercial self-interest, through the use of the headline. In other words, the editor has

(156) abused our language.

Fifth and finally, I wish to point out how some *shukanshi* magazines abuse language and cause serious harm to the affected parties, the readers, and society as a whole. In this regard, three important facts cannot be overlooked. The first is that for some reason or other, these tabloid media sometimes choose particular individuals, groups, or organizations as their prey and try to create false impressions about them by running a long series of articles with highly sensational and misleading headlines. Second, whereas each day millions of Japanese read *shukanshi* magazines, millions more come into contact with their headlines in the advertisements (found, for example, in the major newspapers throughout Japan and on the posters hanging in the commuter trains), and those media, with full knowledge, use their misleading headlines in their advertisements. Third, these magazines often create smoke where there is no fire. As an example, recall the summary of the article under the headline in question.

> (157) *Rumor* is that two female students in Professor Yamamoto's seminar class are on bad terms. This *must* be causing a headache for him.

This shows that the story is far from investigative reporting—in fact, it is nothing more than the reporter's assumptions, based on rumor. (One might even suspect that the rumor itself was created by the reporter.) And this type of "reporting" is one of the standard tactics used by the *shukanshi* magazines).

If we put together these facts with the deliberately misleading headlines these magazines use, we can only conclude that the magazines are guilty of using language as a weapon of harassment—and, moreover, of using it to harass individuals, groups, or organizations they *don't even know*. What they know is that through repeated exposure to their misleading headlines, the public internalizes false images of the victims of the headlines. They know that a lie repeated often enough becomes accepted as truth. They know how to "frame" people, how to brand people with infamy (for example, how to brand "Professor Yamamoto" as a womanizer, sexual harasser, dangerously charismatic professor, evil genius, or whatever) by repeatedly performing suggestive "indirect illocutionary acts."

The headline we are discussing is a symbolic case in which one of the negative functions of human nature has appeared in the form of a linguistic expression and stimulus. We should maintain constant vigilance against this function because it works in an insidious manner. It is hard to recognize, and its influence is not immediately obvious. It creeps into our mind and distorts our thinking and confuses our ability to distinguish between truth and falsehood. While entertained by the implied scandal, we are coaxed to create a false story about the professor, believe it, construct a false memory about the professor, and eventually allow ourselves to have an unreasonable and unjustified antipathy toward him.

This is how this negative function gradually erodes the mind. We should not overlook the true nature of this function. Language is a powerful tool and a double-edged sword. It can be used either to inform or to mislead, to illuminate the truth or distort it, to unite people or divide them. We should never underestimate the power of language. From this perspective, knowing that some may judge me as too harsh, I further submit:

(158) Some *shukanshi* magazines have made a poison
of language and are polluting our internal mental
environment and our society with that poison.

What makes us vulnerable to this "poison"? It is our indifference and apathy. As Pieper (1992) puts it, "The general public is being reduced to a state where people not only are unable to find out about the truth but also become unable even to *search* for the truth because they are satisfied with deception and trickery that have determined their convictions, satisfied with a fictitious reality created by design through the abuse of language." [Italics in original]

Needless to say, the abusers of language do not care about their victims. But it seems that we, too, are becoming insensitive to the linguistic poison and the suffering it can cause the victims and their families. The negative function of human nature not only hooks on to the abuser's insensitivity and indifference but also delights in, and takes advantage of, *our* insensitivity and indifference. In our society, there are many victims of those magazines mentioned above, who are fighting a hard and lonely battle against the forces of linguistic evil.

And their battle is not divorced from us. We should consider it as our own struggle because we, too, are suffering from their negative influence. We said earlier that the human mind is the place for meaning to emerge and become active. To this I would add that the mind, in a sense, is a battleground between positive and negative forces of human nature. The negative side, employing its linguistic weaponry, is attempting at every turn to gain control of the mind and the way that meaning is constructed. If it is simply allowed to run its course, it becomes strong and dominant. Abused language acts as a stimulus to awaken the negative force and induces confusion within us. It is an external environment that, through its influence, becomes an internal, mental environment. The external and internal thus act in concert. On the surface they may seem separate, but they are fundamentally inseparable. At a deeper level, corruption of language leads directly to the deterioration of individual mental health and, eventually, the mental health of society. Therefore, we must struggle against and defeat linguistic evil, which is the externalization of the negative aspect of human nature. Also, the positive and negative are two integral aspects of the same entity in our nature, and so the positive can be strengthened only by facing and conquering the negative.

5

Conclusion: Some Thoughts on Language, Meaning, and Human Nature

At the end of chapter 4, we viewed the human mind as a battleground between positive and negative aspects of human nature. How, then, can we control the negative force instead of permitting it to control us? If the positive and negative are two integral aspects of the same entity in our nature, how can we transform or convert the latter into the former? We may find a hint of an answer in Buddhist philosophy.

The dualistic function of human nature is observed in what are considered positive qualities as well. The maternal instinct, for example, is usually associated with nurturing, life-giving love, but the very power of maternal love can become violent and detrimental. A symbolic example of this is the case of Kishimojin (in Japanese, literally, "Mother of Demon Children"), or Hariti (in Sanskrit), who appears in the Buddhist legend. Kishimojin had hundreds of children. (Depending on the source, the number varies from five hundred to one thousand, and even up to ten thousand.) She doted lovingly on them and made a habit of abducting and killing human babies to feed their flesh to her own children. She symbolizes the negative side of the maternal instinct—the selfish nature of a mother who has a fierce sense of protection for her own children but cares nothing for other children (Ikeda et al. 2003).

According to the legend, the bereaved mothers and other terrified and concerned people begged Shakyamuni for help. To break Kishimojin of her evil ways, Shakyamuni hid her youngest son from her. Although the son was only one of her hundreds of children, she was distraught and sought him desperately throughout the world for seven days. However, she could not find him. She nearly went out of her mind from worry and fear and finally pleaded with Shakyamuni for help. Shakyamuni rebuked her and convinced her to stop killing others' children. Then he returned her son to her. For the first time, Kishimojin realized the suffering and torment that other mothers must have experienced, and vowed to protect all children. In the Dharani chapter of the *Lotus Sutra,* she pledged to protect the votaries of the *Lotus Sutra.* Kishimojin, once an evil demon, then transformed herself into a good demon or Buddhist goddess. In Japan, she is regarded as a goddess of easy delivery and child-rearing.

Demons and gods/goddesses in Buddhism, of course, are not beings but represent functions of human nature. As mentioned earlier, all the qualities or elements that make up human nature exist because they are necessary, and they each have both positive and negative aspects. Anger, for example, cannot be classified as positive or negative. It sometimes produces positive value and sometimes produces negative value. Nor is maternal instinct inherently positive or negative; rather, it has the potential to function either negatively or positively. Positivity and negativity coexist in each element of human nature. They are two potential functions of the same entity.

Now, regarding the transformation of Kishimojin from an evil demon to a benevolent goddess, Ikeda et al. explain:

> (159) The Mother of Demon Children, who dotes lovingly on her own children while not being the least concerned about the children of others, symbolizes the negative side of the maternal instinct. By contrast, to take the love one feels for one's own children and extend it into a love of humanity is the spirit of the merciful mother Perceiver of the World's Sounds, of a bodhisattva.
>
> The Daishonin explains that the name of the "evil demon" Mother of Demon Children can also be read in reverse: "The word *jin* or 'Goddess' represents the ninth consciousness. The word mo or 'Mother' represents the eighth consciousness, the level at which ignorance appears. The word *shi* or 'Children' represents the seventh and sixth consciousnesses. The word *ki* or 'Demon' represents the first five consciousnesses, those of sight, hearing, smell, taste and touch" (Gosho Zenshu 778).
>
> Simply put, the ninth consciousness is the world of Buddhahood. When the world of Buddhahood in the depths of our life wells forth, the eighth (or alaya) consciousness changes, as does the seventh (mano),

136

the sixth (which corresponds to "mind"), and the rest of the five consciousnesses. These are all purified and come to function positively. (Ikeda et al. 2003)

It is beyond both my ability and the scope of this work to explore the theory or concept of the "nine consciousnesses" in depth. Suffice it to say that I do believe that there must be a vast realm of potential lying dormant far beneath our conscious mind.

In chapter 2, we defined the nature of meaning as follows:

(160) Meaning is an emergent phenomenon—it emerges with conditions and disappears with the disappearance of conditions. Thus, it should properly be viewed based on conditioned, or dependent, origination.

And still we are faced with the question, where does meaning, in the broadest sense of the word, ultimately originate? My personal belief is that meaning is omnipresent in the universe and, therefore, one with the universe. In a sense, the universe can be viewed as a great accumulation of semantic energy, from which meanings derive or unfold, and I will call this energy "MEANING" (capitalized to distinguish it from the infinity of meanings that derive from it). Meanings that we perceive are the outwardly manifest aspect of MEANING, but MEANING itself cannot be grasped through any concrete form or image. When MEANING manifests itself, it does so only in response to, and dependent on, the temporary union of conditions—including language and intelligent life such as humans. Also, just as the universe is infinite, so, too, is MEANING.

Understood in this way, the relationship between language and human beings could be described as follows:

> (34) Language is not meaning itself but is one of many different types of stimulus for meaning to emerge and become active, and the human race is one of many possible forms of intelligent life with unknown capacity that can provide a "place" for the activity of meaning.

I now have a feeling that in the MEANING there must be an ultimate source or matrix of the best possible positive meaning. There must be an ultimate "cause" for the most powerful positive meaning to arise. In order to reach the source, bring forth the positive meaning from the source, and have the meaning active in ourselves, we need to tap into, or activate, the "ninth consciousness" in our inner universe, which, I believe, connects and interacts with that ultimate source in the outer universe. In other words, the belief in the ninth consciousness leads to the belief that the human race has the potential to provide the "place" for the activity of the best possible positive meaning and the most powerful positive meaning.

To tap into the ninth consciousness is to draw out all the positive aspects of everything in human nature. Naturally, the great power of that consciousness will manifest in the form of words and actions, in the form of speech acts.

When the ninth consciousness—the enlightened nature of the Buddha—is activated in a person, how would he or she behave? How would he or she act in the midst of reality, where people and their activities are dominated by the other, more superficial layers of consciousness?

Ikeda writes this about the life of the Buddha:

(161) Gautam Buddha did not spend his life attempting to explain a theoretical understanding of the riddle of life, but rather teaching men and women how to overcome suffering and open a path to happiness in the midst of the challenges of life.

Sadly however, this original spirit became obscured and lost over time. Buddhism today is often viewed as a static religion, epitomized by the image of a meditating or sitting Buddha. But a truer image is one of a dynamic, walking Buddha, ceaselessly taking action to lead people to happiness and spiritual freedom.

By examining the life of Gautam Buddha, we can rediscover the essence of his message and tap the spiritual lifeblood of Buddhism that still pulses today. He was a man who pioneered a path of great happiness among the people and who was exceptionally gifted in the art of dialogue. The wisdom and compassion, which characterized his life, are illustrated in the following well-known episodes.

When a mother whose beloved child had died implored the Buddha to revive the child, he told her he could devise a cure if she would bring him a mustard seed. But, he added, this must come from a home that had never known death. The mother began a desperate search, but of course she could find no home which had never lost someone to death. Slowly the grief-stricken mother came to realize that she was not alone in her sorrow, but that every home bore the same burden of bereavement and loss. Thus she determined to overcome her own grief.

Another incident illustrates the essential spirit of Buddhism, where compassion and concrete action to relieve suffering take precedence over abstract theory. One of the Buddha's disciples liked posing philosophical questions, such as, "Is the world infinite or finite?" or "Are the spirit and the physical body one or separate?" Perhaps surprisingly, Gautam would not answer. The disciple became dissatisfied and threatened to leave the Buddhist order.

Gautam replied with the tale of a man who is struck by a poisoned arrow but won't let anyone remove it. He wants first to know who shot the arrow and what the arrow is made of. He continues to ask questions and will not let anyone administer aid until these have been answered, until finally, he dies. The Buddha employed this parable to demonstrate the danger of being obsessed by abstract speculation....

The all-embracing, oceanic compassion of Gautam Buddha is the perfect model. His message was that compassionate action is the fundamental purpose of human life, and that it is by working to fulfill this mission that we can enjoy lives of genuine meaning. His philosophy not only has the power to transform our thinking, it also leads to hope and practical action and unleashes a powerful energy for living. As we translate it into practice, our personal drama of self-reformation begins. And that reformation of the individual spurs reformation on every level. It is the first turn of the wheel in the process to make humanity strong and wise. (Ikeda 2003)

As is generally known, the Buddha himself did not leave any written records. His teachings were originally transmitted orally before they were written down for the first time in the first century B.C. (some five centuries after his death). This is why many Buddhist sutras begin with the phrase *nyoze gamon* (in Japanese, "This is what I heard," or "Thus have I heard") or *evam mayashrutam* (in Sanskrit).

As a student of linguistics, I feel that while the teachings of the Buddha are for all humanity and not just for the people of his time and place, his actual *words* were not abstract. They must have been uttered based on his strong, single-minded, and compassionate determination to help the men and women in front of him to "overcome suffering and open a path to happiness in the midst of the challenges of life" (Ikeda 2003). For him language was a means to perform his compassionate illocutionary acts of "leading people to happiness and spiritual freedom" (Ikeda 2003). And the wisdom arising from his compassion enabled him to become a true "master of words." Deeply considering the case of each individual, through his illocutionary acts, direct or indirect, he tenaciously and tirelessly tried to stimulate and unleash the unlimited potential that is dormant in the people's inner universe.

Shakyamuni Buddha, who discovered his cosmic self, carried out his mission of compassion as the "Teacher of Humanity," making unflagging efforts to eventually awaken people to the ninth consciousness, which lies at the utmost depths of their being.

If the ninth consciousness, which the Buddha perceived in his being, is innate in every human being, it follows that the "cause" enabling us to realize the ultimate *meaning* of our existence also lies deep within us. And that great realization should, in turn, enable us to realize why we were born the way we are and to find out how we should get the most out of life. It should lead to the great discovery and realization of our mission in life.

But then, how can we *realize* the meaning of our existence? It does not seem to be a matter of intellectual grasp.

The Buddha's "message was that compassionate action is the fundamental purpose of human life, and that it is by working to fulfill this mission that we can enjoy lives of genuine meaning" (Ikeda 2003). This implies that realization and action coincide. We tend to assume that realization precedes action, but that assumption would make us fall into the same trap as did the disciple of the Buddha who liked posing philosophical questions.

The real question is, how can we realize the meaning of our existence *with the entirety of our being?*

The Buddha left his teachings for all humanity. His message was intended not only for his contemporaries but for all future generations. The question is, why did the "original spirit," or the ultimate *intended meaning,* of his teachings become "obscured and lost over time" (Ikeda 2003)?

Recall what we said about the emergence of meaning in chapter 2: (1) Meaning is an *emergent* phenomenon—it emerges with conditions and disappears when the conditions disappear. (2) Meaning arises in response to, and dependent on, the *temporary union* of conditions (including language and a person). And (3) language is not meaning in itself but is one of many different types of stimulus for meaning to emerge and become active, and the human race is one of many possible forms of intelligent life with an unknown capacity to provide a *place* for the activity of meaning.

The Buddha dedicated his life to serve as a great "condition" and passed away about 2,500 years ago. Probably, during his life and for some time after his death, there was the temporary union of conditions that supported the emergence of the Buddha's intended meaning. Even if the period had extended for hundreds of years or more, it was nonetheless "temporary" in that it eventually disintegrated over time.

After the disintegration of the temporary union of conditions mentioned above, what happened to the Buddha's intended meaning? It continued to exist as a potential.

The historical Buddha (Prince Siddhartha, later Gautama Buddha), who was a great condition, ceased to exist 2,500 years ago, but his teachings survived in the form of the sutras. In other words, the way for people to gain access to the great condition was through the sutras.

But the Buddha's teachings in the form of the sutras, or written compositions, are not "meaning" in themselves. They are one of the conditions for his intended meaning to emerge and become active, and in the absence of the right "perceiver," the meaning just exists with the texts in the state of potentiality.

I believe that the words of any truly great teacher of humanity, including those of the Buddha, originate in his or her ninth consciousness. The true intended meaning of such words exists as a potential with the words.

I also believe that this fundamental pure consciousness called the ninth consciousness lies in the depths of every human being. Therefore, each of us is a potential perceiver of the above-mentioned meaning.

The conditions that enable the best possible and most powerful positive meaning to emerge and become active exist as potentials in the depths of those words and our being. The most fundamental question to ask is how the potential meaning is actualized.

The ninth consciousness is something that illuminates the entirety of our inner universe, and so, when one reads the words from the ninth consciousness, one must do so with one's whole being. They are not words that can be read by exercising intelligent reasoning alone or that can be discussed at a merely theoretical level.

And if one perceives the true message of those words, that great realization will lead directly to compassionate action. The perceiver will devote body and soul to serve as a condition for activating the ninth consciousness of the people who are "in the midst of the challenges of life." In other words, their compassionate action is the proof of their having perceived the true intended meaning.

Meaning is an emergent phenomenon. It is not something that can be transplanted from one person's mind to another's. The best possible and most powerful positive meaning also wells forth from deep within ourselves, coinciding with the temporary union of conditions—namely, our earnest seeking mind, language of true wisdom, and the one who has perceived the meaning with his or her whole being.

References

Anderson, Richard C., Ralph E. Reynolds, Diane L. Schallert, and Ernest T. Goetz. 1977. "Frameworks for Comprehending Discourse." *American Educational Research Journal* 14 (4): 367–82.

Anderson, Richard C., and Zohara Shifrin. 1980. "The Meaning of Words in Context." In *Theoretical Issues in Reading Comprehension,* ed. Rand Spiro, Bertram Bruce, and William Brewer, 331–48. Hillsdale, N.J.: Lawrence Erlbaum.

Aristotle. 1941. "Poetics." In *The Basic Works of Aristotle,* ed. Richard McKeon, trans. Ingram Bywater, 1453–87. New York: Random House.

Asahi Evening News. 1992. "Dahmer: 'I Know Society Will Never Forgive Me.'" Tokyo, February 18.

Asher, Nicholas, and Alex Lascarides. 2003. *Logics of Conversation.* Cambridge, UK: Cambridge University Press.

Austin, John L. 1962. *How to Do Things with Words.* Oxford, UK: Oxford University Press.

Bach, Kent. 2001. "Speaking Loosely: Sentence Nonliterality." *Midwest Studies in Philosophy* 25 (1): 249–63.

———. 2002. "Seemingly Semantic Intuitions." In *Meaning and Truth,* ed. Joseph K. Campbell, Michael O'Rourke, and David Shier, 21–33. New York: Seven Bridges Press.

Bande, Usha. 2003. "I Feel Strongly More than Words, an Attitude." *Tribune* Online Edition, July 27, www. tribuneindia.com/2003/20030727/herworld.htm (accessed November 16, 2008).

Blamires, Mike. 1999. "Dazzled by the Spectrum: Where Should We Be Looking?" http://trainland.tripod.com/mike. htm (accessed December 26, 2006).

Bower, Gordon H., John B. Black, and Terrence J. Turner. 1979. "Scripts in Memory for Text." *Cognitive Psychology* 11: 177–220.

Bransford, John D., and Marcia K. Johnson. 1972. "Contextual Prerequisites for Understanding: Some Investigations of Comprehension and Recall." *Journal of Verbal Learning and Verbal Behavior* 11: 717–26.

Brown, Gillian, and George Yule. 1983. *Discourse Analysis*. Cambridge, UK: Cambridge University Press.

Brussat, Frederic, and Mary A. Brussat. 1988. Review of *Working Girl* (20th Century Fox film) in "Spirituality and Practice," www.spiritualityandpractice.com/films/films. php?id=2750 (accessed November 11, 2008).

Carroll, Noël. 2001. "On the Narrative Connection." In *New Perspectives on Narrative Perspective,* ed. Willie van Peer and Seymour Chatman, 21–41. Albany, N.Y.: State University of New York Press.

Central Queensland University. 2001. "Module 8 Narrative," http://webfuse.cqu.edu.au/Courses/win2001/ COMM11005/Resources/Lectures/Module_8/ (accessed November 16, 2008).

Chandler, Daniel. 1997. "Visual Perception," www.aber.ac.uk/ media/Modules/MC10220/ (accessed November 16, 2008).

Chua, Kao-Ping. 2006. "Introduction to Framing." American Medical Student Association, www.amsa.org/uhc/FramingIntro.pdf. (accessed November 16, 2008).

Clark, Wesley. 1999. The Analysis, Observation and Documentation of Missing Time and Information within Written Statements, http://truthsleuth.com/Missing%20Time%20and%20Information.htm (accessed January 1, 2007).

Dodd, David H., and Jeffrey M. Bradshaw. 1980. "Leading Questions and Memory: Pragmatic Constraints." *Journal of Verbal Learning and Verbal Behavior* 19: 695–704.

Dyer, Michael G., Margot Flowers, and Yih-Jih A. Wang. 1992. "Distributed Symbol Discovery through Symbol Recirculation: Toward Natural Language Processing in Distributed Connectionist Networks." In *Connectionist Approaches to Natural Language Understanding,* ed. Ronan Reilly and Noel Sharkey, 21–48, www.cs.ucla.edu/~dyer/Papers/DistSymDisc/DistSymDisc92.html (accessed November 12, 2008).

Fisher, Walter. 1987. *Human Communication as Narration: Toward a Philosophy of Reason, Value, and Action.* Columbia, S.C.: University of South Carolina Press.

Forster, Edward. M. 1927. *Aspects of the Novel.* New York: Harcourt Brace.

Garrod, Simon. 1985. "Incremental Pragmatic Interpretation versus Occasional Inferencing during Fluent Reading." In *Inferences in Text Processing,* ed. Gert Rickheit and Hans Strohner, 161–81. Amsterdam: North-Holland.

Gasser, Michael. 2003. "How Language Works," www.indiana.edu/~hlw/Introduction/themes.html (accessed August 24, 2006).

Gerrie, Matthew P., Maryanne Garry, and Elizabeth F. Loftus. 2005. "False Memories." In *Psychology and Law: An Empirical Perspective,* ed. Neil Brewer and Kipling Williams, 222–53. New York: Guilford Press.

Grice, Herbert P. 1975. "Logic and Conversation." In *Syntax and Semantics,* vol. 3: *Speech Acts,* ed. Peter Cole and Jerry L. Morgan, 41–58. New York: Academic Press.

———. 1989. *Studies in the Way of Words.* Cambridge, Mass.: Harvard University Press.

Hamann, Cornelia. 1989. "English Temporal Clauses in a Reference Frame Model." In *Essays on Tensing in English,* vol. 2: *Time, Text and Modality,* ed. Alfred Schopf, 31–154. Tübingen, Germany: Niemeyer.

Hawkins, John A. 1978. *Definiteness and Indefiniteness: A Study in Reference and Grammaticality Prediction.* London: Croom Helm.

Herman, David. 2000. "Narratology as a Cognitive Science." *IMAGE & NARRATIVE* (Online Magazine of the Visual Narrative), www.imageandnarrative.be/narratology/davidherman.htm (accessed November 17, 2008).

Ikeda, Daisaku. 2003. "A Human Revolution." *Life Positive Plus* (Buddhist magazine published in India), October–December 2003, www.lifepositive.com/Spirit/Buddhism/Human_Revolution.asp (accessed November 17, 2008).

Ikeda, Daisaku, Katsuji Saito, Takanori Endo, and Haruo Suda. 2002. *The Wisdom of the Lotus Sutra: A Discussion,* vol. 4. Santa Monica, Calif.: World Tribune Press.

———. 2003. *The Wisdom of the Lotus Sutra: A Discussion,* vol. 6. Santa Monica, Calif.: World Tribune Press.

Jahn, Manfred. 2005. "Narratology: A Guide to the Theory of Narrative," www.uni-koeln.de/~ame02/pppn.htm (accessed November 17, 2008).

Keller, Helen. 1903. *The Story of My Life.* New York: Doubleday, Page.

Kitchell, Kenneth F. 2000. "Latin III's Dirty Little Secret—Why Johnny Can't Read." *New England Classical Newsletter* 27: 206–26, http://pvclassics.org/index2.php?option=com_content&do_pdf=1&id=12 (accessed August 15, 2006).

Lakoff, George. 2004a. "Simple Framing," www.rockridgeinstitute.org/projects/strategic/simple_framing (accessed November 17, 2008).

———. 2004b. *Don't Think of an Elephant! Know Your Values and Frame the Debate. The Essential Guide for Progressives.* White River Junction, Vt.: Chelsea Green.

Law, Stephen. 2003. *The Philosophy Gym: 25 Short Adventures in Thinking.* New York: St. Martin's Press, http://virtualatdp.berkeley.edu:8081/philosophy/_2/_/1 (accessed Nov. 2, 2008).

Lebedev, Artemy. 2006. "Mandership," www.artlebedev.com/mandership/136 (accessed November 17, 2008).

Loftus, Elizabeth, and John Palmer. 1974. "Reconstruction of Automobile Destruction: An Example of the Interaction between Language and Memory." *Journal of Verbal Learning and Verbal Behavior,* 13 (5): 585–89.

The Lotus Sutra. 1993. Trans. Burton Watson. New York: Columbia University Press.

McKoon, Gail, and Roger Ratcliff. 1992. "Inference during Reading." *Psychological Review* 99 (3): 440–66.

Merriam-Webster. 2003. *Merriam-Webster's 11th Collegiate Dictionary.* Springfield, Mass.: Merriam-Webster.

Mori, Yoshinobu. 1987. *Hashiwatashi Eibunpo.* Tokyo: Taishukan.

Nichiren. 1999. *The Writings of Nichiren Daishonin.* Trans. and ed. Gosho Translation Committee. Tokyo: Soka Gakkai.

Norvig, Peter. 1987. "Inference in Text Understanding." In *Proceedings of the Sixth National Conference on Artificial Intelligence,* 561–65. Seattle: American Association for Artificial Intelligence (AAAI) Press, www.norvig.com/aaai87.pdf (accessed November 11, 2008).

Oberlander, Jon, and Alex Lascarides. 2000. "Laconic Discourses and Total Eclipses: Abduction in DICE." In *Abduction, Beliefs and Context in Dialogue: Studies in Computational Pragmatics,* ed. Harry Bunt and William Black, 391–412. Amsterdam: John Benjamins, www.cogsci.ed.ac.uk/~alex/papers/laconic.ps (accessed November 17, 2008).

O'Brien, Edna. 1980. *Mrs. Reinhardt and Other Stories.* New York: Penguin.

Pieper, Josef. 1992. *Abuse of Language, Abuse of Power.* Trans. Lothar Krauth. San Francisco: Ignatius Press.

Quirk, Randolph, Sidney Greenbaum, Geoffrey Leech, and Jan Svartvik. 1985. *A Comprehensive Grammar of the English Language.* London: Longman.

Reid, Gordon. 2001. "The Place of Meaning," http://pandora.nla.gov.au/pan/14033/20010108-0000/jacobyte/The_Place_of_Meaning.pdf (accessed November 18, 2008).

Reynolds, Ralph. 2002. "Understanding the Nature of Reading Comprehension: Basic Research and Instructional Implications," www.sprakaloss.se/reinolds englich.htm (accessed November 16, 2008).

Rosenhan, David. L. 1973. "On Being Sane in Insane Places." *Science* 179: 250–58.

Ruhl, Charles. 1989. *On Monosemy: A Study in Linguistic Semantics*. Albany, N.Y.: State University of New York Press.

Schank, Roger C., and Robert P. Abelson. 1977. "Scripts, Plans, and Knowledge." In *Thinking: Readings in Cognitive Science*, ed. Philip N. Johnson-Laird and Peter C. Wason, 421–32. Cambridge, UK: Cambridge University Press.

Searle, John R. 1979. *Expression and Meaning: Studies in the Theory of Speech Acts*. Cambridge, UK: Cambridge University Press.

Smith, Edward E., and David A. Swinney. 1992. "The Role of Schemas in Reading Text: A Real-Time Examination." *Discourse Processes* 15 (3): 303–16, http://lcnl.ucsd.edu/ LCNL_main_page/Publications_PDF/1992_Smith_ Swinney.pdf. (accessed November 18, 2008).

Sweetser, Eve. 1990. *From Etymology to Pragmatics: Metaphorical and Cultural Aspects of Semantic Structure*. Cambridge, UK: Cambridge University Press.

Takahashi, Takenori. 2003. "Teaching English with Movie Scenes: Case Study—Opening Scene of *Working Girl*." *Journal of Language and Culture,* Toyo University, 3: 21–32.

———. 2006. "Four-Stage Pedagogical Approach to Speech-Act Conjunction." *Dialogos: Proceedings of the Department of English Communication*, Toyo University, 6: 161–71.

Velleman, James David. 2002. "Narrative Explanation,"
www.law.berkeley.edu/centers/kadish/Velleman%20
NARRATIVE.pdf (accessed November 18, 2008).

———. 2003. "Narrative Explanation." *Philosophical Review*
112 (1): 2003.

Wickramasinghe, Chandra. 2000. "A Panspermic View of Life:
Interview with N. Chandra Wickramasinghe." *Frontline*
17 (25), www.hinduonnet.com/fline/fl1725/17250800.htm
(accessed November 18, 2008).

Wittgenstein, Ludwig. 2001. *Philosophical Investigations,* 3rd
ed., trans. G. E. M. Anscombe. Oxford, UK: Blackwell.

Worth, Sarah. 2005. "Narrative Knowledge: Knowing through
Storytelling," web.mit.edu/comm-forum/mit4/papers/
worth.pdf (accessed November 18, 2008).

Zhao, Wuming. 1996. "Cinderella in Eighties' Hollywood,"
www.cmn.hs.h.kyoto-u.ac.jp/NO1/SUBJECT2/CIN.HTM
(accessed November 18, 2008).

Ziff, Paul. 1972. "What Is Said." In *Semantics of Natural
Language,* ed. Donald Davidson and Gilbert Harman,
709–21. Dordrecht, Netherlands: Reidel.

Index

A

ability, tendency, and motivation to
  develop a story 57
abstract meaning 9
abstractness 10
accident occurring at a high speed
  frame 124
accident occurring at a low speed
  frame 123
activate 10, 11, 23, 82, 138, 139
activated associations 117
activation 11, 20, 23, 124
activation of the schema 84
active mental process 56
active participant in the production
  of meaning 64
act of informing 110
act of lying 118
act of producing and communicating written text 116
act of proposing 112
act performed in the production
  and communication of the
  written text 116

actualization 23, 32, 125, 128
actualization of meaning
  potentials 26, 125
actualization of the meaning
  potential of a text 29
actualize 26, 28, 29, 31, 32, 97, 102,
  125, 144
actualizing the meaning potentials
  of language 28
advertisements 130
agent 10
agent argument 10
ambiguity 3
annals 74
antecedent (or attendant, or supportive) conditions 29
appetite for scandal 128
arguments of "kick" 10
arising and cessation of
  meaning 22
arising of meaning 25
aspects of "bark" 18
asserting 113, 114, 115
assertion 118, 119

outer universe   138
outwardly manifest aspect of
     MEANING   44, 137

P

panspermic view of life   45
paraphrasing   10
partial completion   55
passive recipient   64
perceiver(s)   18, 19, 143, 144
perceiver as condition   19
perception   12, 52, 59
perceptual experience   54
perceptually modify   54
perceptual transitions   54
phatic   108
phonetic   108
place for narrative to emerge   77
place for the activity of
     meaning   44, 47, 72, 138, 143
polysemy   9
positive and negative aspects of
     human nature   134
positive and negative forces of
     human nature   133
positive value   136
positivity   136
possible deception   119
possible meanings   5, 23, 24, 128
potential(s)   18, 21, 23, 125, 136, 137,
     138, 141, 143, 144
potential as a story   97
potentiality   143
potential meaning   25, 144
potential perceiver   144
power of language   6, 7, 132
pragmatic   103

pragmatically   104
pragmatics   104, 105
pragmatist(s)   104
preconceived assumption   28, 31
prefix   109
Prince Siddhartha   143
principle of closure   54, 56
principle of contiguity (or
     proximity)   53
principle of proximity   58
prior experience and knowl-
     edge   82
production of meaning   81
profound reader   99
profound reading   100
promising   115
propensity for story-making   52,
     59
propositional content   110

Q

quality of a gestalt   58
questions of abstract theory and
     ideology   101

R

reader's knowledge   13
reader's memory   124
readers' interests and prior
     experience   128
reality   98, 100, 102
receiving and responding to
     linguistic stimuli   28
recipient   125
recipient of the linguistic
     stimuli   26